SEPARATE LIVES

ALSO BY SILVIA PETTEM

In Search of the Blonde Tigress: The Untold Story of Eleanor Jarman

Someone's Daughter: In Search of Justice for Jane Doe, Updated Edition

Cold Case Chronicles: Mysteries, Murders & the Missing

The Long Term Missing: Hope and Help for Families

Cold Case Research: Resources for Unidentified, Missing, and Cold Homicide Cases

Only in Boulder: The County's Colorful Characters

Boulder: A Sense of Time and Place, Revisited

Positively Pearl Street: A Chronicle of the Center of Boulder, Colorado, 1859 to Present

Inn and Around Nederland: Accommodating the Traveler, Then and Now

Excursions From Peak to Peak: Then and Now

Boulder: Evolution of a City

SEPARATE LIVES

Uncovering the Hidden Family of
Victorian Professor Mary Rippon

SILVIA PETTEM

Foreword by Julia Bricklin

LYONS
PRESS

Essex, Connecticut

An imprint of Globe Pequot, the trade division of
The Rowman & Littlefield Publishing Group, Inc.
4501 Forbes Blvd., Ste. 200
Lanham, MD 20706
www.rowman.com

Distributed by NATIONAL BOOK NETWORK

British Library Cataloguing in Publication Information available

Library of Congress Cataloging-in-Publication Data
Names: Pettem, Silvia, author.
Title: Separate lives : uncovering the hidden family of Victorian professor Mary Rippon / Silvia
    Pettem ; foreword by Julia Bricklin.
Description: First Lyons Press edition. | Essex, Connecticut : Lyons Press, [2024] | First edition
    published in 1999. | Includes bibliographical references and index.
Identifiers: LCCN 2023058938 (print) | LCCN 2023058939 (ebook) | ISBN 9781493079353
    (cloth : acid-free paper) | ISBN 9781493079360 (epub)
Subjects: LCSH: Rippon, Mary, 1850-1935. | Women educators—Colorado—Boulder—
    Biography. | University of Colorado, Boulder—History. | Divorced mothers—Colorado—
    Boulder—Biography. | Mothers and daughters.
Classification: LCC LA2317.R54 P48 2024 (print) | LCC LA2317.R54 (ebook) | DDC 370.92
    [B]—dc23/eng/20240222
LC record available at https://lccn.loc.gov/2023058938
LC ebook record available at https://lccn.loc.gov/2023058939

∞™ The paper used in this publication meets the minimum requirements of American National
Standard for Information Sciences—Permanence of Paper for Printed Library Materials, ANSI/
NISO Z39.48-1992.

To Mary's only grandchild, Wilfred Rieder,
who knew her story needed to be told.

CONTENTS

List of Illustrations

LIST OF CHARACTERS

Bell, Delphine, University of Colorado instructor and lifelong friend of Mary Rippon

Bell, Dr. James Washington, University of Colorado professor

Bell, Rosetta, daughter of Delphine and Dr. James Washington Bell

Brackett, Dr. J. Raymond, University of Colorado professor and lifelong friend of Mary Rippon

Brackett, Lottie, wife of Raymond Brackett

Housel, William "Will" C., husband of Mary Rippon

Ingersoll, Dr. Ross, student of Miriam Rieder

Litsey, John, third childhood guardian of Mary Rippon

Massey, Miriam Barstow, childhood friend of Mary Rippon

Rieder, Eric, great-grandson of Mary Rippon and Will Housel

Rieder, Miriam Edna Housel, daughter of Mary Rippon and Will Housel

Rieder, Rudolf, husband of Miriam Edna Housel

Rieder, Wilfred (Walfried Wolf), son of Miriam and Rudolf Rieder

Rippon, Jane Skinner, mother of Mary Rippon

Rippon, Thomas, father of Mary Rippon

Searles, Dora Mae (Dorothy), second wife of William "Will" C. Housel

Sewall, Addie, daughter of Joseph Sewall

Sewall, Joseph, first president of the University of Colorado

Skinner, Hannah Alford ("Auntie"), aunt of Mary Rippon

Skinner, William Sr., grandfather and first guardian of Mary Rippon

Skinner, William W. ("Uncle"), uncle and second guardian of Mary Rippon

von Brandis, Anna, close friend, in Germany, of Mary Rippon

Whitney, Norman W., second husband of Jane Skinner Rippon

Whitney, Norman. R., nephew of Mary Rippon

Whitney, Omar, half-brother of Mary Rippon

Foreword

I met Silvia Pettem some years ago when our publisher introduced us. We both wrote books that feature female criminals who, in 1933, were caught up in America's obsession with gangs, alcohol, and the unraveling nuclear family, as well as in the resulting sensational media coverage. Pettem's subject lived in Chicago; mine in Los Angeles. Other than that, their stories were remarkably similar. Both of our subjects were accomplices to murder or attempted murder, perpetrated by their love interests. The press greatly exaggerated their involvement, dubbing them "The Blonde Tigress" and "The Blonde Rattlesnake."

So, when Silvia told me she was re-publishing her book about a pioneer woman educator, I was intrigued. Was Mary Rippon another woman in history who struggled to reclaim her identity? Was she impoverished? A victim of a romantic relationship gone bad?

Turns out, Rippon was none of these things. Instead, she was one of the first women to enter academia, a field that had been held predominantly by men for hundreds of years. Her employer, the University of Colorado in Boulder, led change in this regard. Its founders wrote into its constitution a mandate to teach men and women equally. Rippon joined the faculty in 1878 as an instructor, becoming the first woman there to teach and one of the first in the nation to teach at a state university. She worked her way up to become the first female professor, and eventually, chair of the Department of German language and literature. She was all these things before she could even vote.

But this success came with a price. In the nineteenth and early twentieth century, society didn't allow women with professional careers to have families. Rippon defied this convention, but she had to do so in secret. More potentially scandalous, she fell in love with one of her students and became pregnant with his child. In what appears to have been an incredible feat of maternal selflessness, she allowed her younger, less-established husband to divorce her and raise their child overseas and then in another state, even as he started another family with another woman. Rippon even supported his new family financially, doing whatever she could to maintain respectability for their daughter.

Rippon directly and indirectly ushered in a new era of female academics in Boulder and the nation at large. But to do this, she had to subvert the exhaustion brought on by leading two distinctly separate lives: one public, one private. For reasons exquisitely told in Pettem's narrative, the professor chose not to tell her own daughter of their real relationship until circumstances forced her to do so, and even then, she kept the truth from all but two very close friends.

Just as Pettem did with *In Search of the Blonde Tigress: The Untold Story of Eleanor Jarman*, she weaves her meticulous research into a fast-paced, historical narrative. *Separate Lives: Uncovering the Hidden Family of Victorian Professor Mary Rippon* is a story about a woman who never intended to be a trailblazer but, like so many other women then and now, had to sacrifice personal happiness and work thrice as hard to ensure the safety and the emotional and material well-being of her child. And yet, if readers are looking for martyrdom or regret, they won't find it here. "Conventionality is the mother of dreariness," Rippon once wrote, no doubt a nod to the complicated life she led, even as she comported to norms in public.

Readers will have to make up their own minds about motherhood, career, and achievement, and whether we've come far enough in supporting modern-day Mary Rippons.

—Julia Bricklin, author of *The Red Sapphire:*
The Woman Who Beat the Blacklist

INTRODUCTION

My interest in Mary Rippon began in late 1993 in the small basement room in Norlin Library on the Boulder campus that houses the University of Colorado's archives. Because I had expressed an interest in the Victorian era and in women's history, the librarian suggested that I might wish to look at some unusual information about Mary Rippon. To Boulder residents, Mary Rippon is the familiar name of the university's outdoor theater where Shakespeare's plays are performed every summer. Despite the widespread use of her name, however, few people know that Mary Rippon chaired the German department as the university's first female professor. And even those who knew of her position assumed until fairly recently that up until her death in 1935, she had led a quiet, scholarly, spinster's life.

When I studied her photographs in old yearbooks, a plain, gentle-looking woman stared back at me—but I soon discovered that "Miss Rippon," as she was called, took extraordinary steps to clothe part of her life in secrecy. In fact, her private life would have been considered scandalous at the time, and because of that she kept a low profile during her distinguished thirty-one-year career—never involved in controversy, always praised in the local press.

The historical view of the perfect Miss Rippon was altered suddenly in February 1976 when an elderly man from the East Coast made his way down the steps to the archives and donated two photographs to the university. Although the items in this first donation were unrelated to Mary Rippon, the man identified himself to a *Colorado Alumnus* reporter as "Wilfred Rieder, a descendant of Mary Rippon." The article caused a minor uproar among librarians, faculty, and long-time Boulder residents.

How could the never-married "Miss Rippon" have a descendant? At that time there were no known records or documentation of a secret life.

Before his death in 1986, Wilfred Rieder made a second donation—this time of Mary's plain leather diaries, journals, and account books. He also explained to a reporter of *Summit Magazine* (another alumni publication) that he was Mary Rippon's grandson. This time he gave more details and stated that in 1888, Mary had entered into a romantic relationship with one of her students and had become pregnant. She married secretly, gave birth to a baby girl during a year's sabbatical in Germany, then returned to Colorado and resumed her teaching career as if nothing had changed.

Mary's diaries are cryptic, with only a sentence or two for each day. Her entries are written in delicate handwriting and often consist of a phrase such as "Went to Mrs. Bell's" or a brief notation on the weather. Rarely did Mary state her feelings, but the few times she did were revealing.

The account books, however, provided much more detailed information. For many years Mary itemized all of her expenses, leaving clues about her day-to-day lifestyle, her priorities, and her heavy financial responsibilities. In her journals, Mary listed the letters she wrote and received.

After the library accepted Wilfred's valuable donations, they lay untouched for want of a researcher with time to delve into Mary's story—until the sharp contrast between the difficulties in Mary's private life and her achievements in public life drew me into the mystery of her story. A few months of historical detective work turned into a five-year compulsion. The first edition of *Separate Lives* became an all-consuming research project that nagged at me month after month and year after year until it pushed all other projects aside.

During this time, I expanded my search to property and guardianship records. I read brittle newspapers from the nineteenth century, collected old photographs and legal documents, and carefully dissected the phrases in Mary's diaries. I spent hours and hours tracking anyone and everyone who had a connection to her story. The more I discovered, the more fascinated I became.

Mary did not fit into the narrowly defined role assigned to women in Victorian society. She excelled in the male world of academia without blemishing her feminine image. A state legislator praised both Mary's knowledge and her teaching ability. She was venerated by her students, who equated her with German playwright Goethe's vision of the "woman eternal."

Yet in her private life, Mary rejected what was known in Victorian times as the "woman's sphere." She did not stay at home with her family, although, in her own way, she became involved in her family's affairs. To keep her job, she hid her husband and child behind a curtain of secrecy throughout her lifetime.

No other books have been published about Mary Rippon. *Separate Lives* interweaves her private life with her professional career and tells the whole story for the first time. My purpose is not to tarnish her well-deserved reputation, but rather to uncover the human side of a woman whose circumstances clashed with the mores of her times. Her life was her own, as free as her wildflower garden—an anomaly in an otherwise structured world.

Since the letters and diaries that might have detailed the beginnings of Mary's love affair and her feelings about them—as well as the subsequent pregnancy and marriage—are not available, it is tempting to imagine events and feelings. However, the evidence in the account books of Mary's lifelong acceptance of her responsibility toward her husband and their child, and the few poignant verses tucked into other diaries, are more eloquent than anything one might imagine.

Often, I am asked if Mary's life was fulfilling or tragic. Was she happy with her accomplishments, or did she consider herself a victim? Readers have their own opinions about motherhood, career, and achievement and will have to form their own conclusions. Balancing a family and a career is still difficult, but it is acceptable, and often applauded, in the United States. However, sexual relationships between a professor and a student are not applauded and currently require full disclosure. If that had been the case for Mary, it's likely that her love affair never would have happened. If her marriage could have been publicly revealed without loss of her job, however, Mary might have been acknowledged as a mother as well as a teacher. Such speculations, though, are not to the point. For Mary Rippon, combining a family and a career was impossible.

A researcher usually starts with the latest information about a life and traces that life backwards in time. When I had found as much as I could about Mary's adult life, I set out to learn what I could of her childhood. I wanted to learn what events in her past had shaped her future. I needed to start at the beginning, so I flew from Colorado to Chicago and drove southwest to Kendall County, Illinois.

Before I left, I had practically memorized the county road map. On the plane I kept it and a state map open in front of me. As the plane neared Chicago, I followed rivers and highways to get my bearings. After crossing the Illinois River, the plane flew quite low. Suddenly, I recognized roads, communities, and even the Lisbon Cemetery where I hoped I would find Mary's relatives. I breathed a sigh of relief as I saw cornfields and not shopping centers, in the rural countryside.

After a search of Mary's family's property records in the county courthouse, I discovered the location of her father's farm. It was there, in the middle of the nineteenth century, that Mary Rippon was born.

Silvia Pettem

PART 1

EARLY YEARS, 1850–1877

CHAPTER 1

IN THE NEARLY TREELESS EXPANSE OF NORTHEASTERN ILLINOIS, 1833 was known as "the year of the early spring." The snow had melted in February, and by early March, warm weather forced open the leaves of the few trees and shrubs along streams and rivers. By the end of the month, the first farmers in the area grazed their stock on the open prairie as yellow primroses and dark blue spiderwort burst into bloom.

Soldiers returning to the eastern states from the Black Hawk War had spoken highly of the slightly undulating land with its rich black soil. There were few stumps or stones to slow down the plows of New York and New England farmers. The Indians had been pushed west of the Mississippi River, and the area now known as Kendall County was open for settlement.

Soon, small farmers from the East arrived with their families in search of a better economic future. With them came their values and ideals. Many who moved to Kendall County, Illinois, were from Oneida County in central upstate New York. Beginning in the 1830s, this Oneida community had become a center for religious revival and social reform. The recently opened Oneida Institute of Science and Industry favored women's rights, temperance, and prison reform, but its main cause was the emancipation of slaves. The Anti-Slavery Society, which spread throughout the North, originated in this same area in 1831. Staunch abolitionists initiated a pamphlet campaign urging the immediate end to slavery, which they opposed purely on moral grounds.

Groups of like-minded New York families journeyed west together to escape the conflict. Illinois had been admitted to the Union as a free state, although many settlers in the southern sections still favored slavery.

Abolitionists relocated in tight-knit groups in the northern part of the state. About twenty farming families from Oneida County left New York in 1835 and 1836 to form the Lisbon Colony in what is now Kendall County, Illinois.

Their journey was relatively easy. Farmers loaded their belongings onto flatboats that were pulled westward along the Erie Canal. In Buffalo, New York, the families boarded steamers for the five- or six-day voyage across Lake Erie and Lake Huron to Lake Michigan, where they debarked at the port of Chicago.

Horse-drawn wagons carried the farmers, their families, and their farming equipment and household goods to Kendall County on the Chicago-to-Ottawa, or High Prairie, Trail. In 1838, surveyors divided Illinois into townships and sections. Grids were formed with north–south and east–west boundaries. Settlers who had already cultivated their land were granted a preemption. Newcomers purchased land from the federal government for one dollar and twenty-five cents per acre.

As family after family left their old farms in New York State, others arrived to take their places. In 1834, the William Skinners of Devonshire, England, in their own search for a better life, crossed the Atlantic Ocean with their three children. When they arrived, they purchased farmland in Sangerfield, Oneida County, New York. Daughter Jane Skinner was nine years old at the time, and her brother William was six.

The Skinners had six more children during the twelve years they lived in New York. Then they, too, decided to join the western movement to Kendall County, Illinois. When the family arrived in Illinois in the summer of 1846, daughter Jane was twenty-one years old.

Jane's father, William Skinner Sr., purchased one hundred and sixty acres in the small community of Lisbon Center, so-named because it was located in the center of Lisbon Township in Kendall County. Twenty-six-year-old Thomas Rippon, another English native, had purchased forty acres of farmland a few months before their arrival. He may have been a former neighbor in New York. In Kendall County, his property was one mile west of the Skinners's farm on Lisbon Center Road.

Thomas Rippon chose the top of a slight ridge for his log cabin. It was there that he took his bride, Jane Skinner. They probably married in 1849, as they expected their first child the following spring.

Mary Ann Rippon was born on May 25, 1850. Her first view of the world included corn and wheat fields in every direction. The barnyard held a few sheep kept for their wool as well as the family's milk cow, a new calf, a horse, and a new colt. Aunts, uncles, and grandparents lived just down the road.

After the arrival of their first child, life in the Rippon home changed a second time. During the 1850 fall harvest, Thomas became weak and tired easily. Twenty-five-year-old Jane divided her time between spinning and weaving, cooking and cleaning, caring for Mary, and nursing her ailing husband. Thomas's condition worsened throughout the winter. According to probate records, the thirty-one-year-old husband and father died of typhoid fever on March 27, 1851, without making out a will.

Figure 1.1. Although Thomas Rippon's gravestone had settled by the time this photo was taken in 1998, the inscription was still legible.
PHOTO BY AUTHOR

Thomas's body was placed in a coffin in the Rippon cabin, transferred to a horse-drawn wagon, and taken to the small prairie Lisbon Cemetery for burial. Besides a few Bible verses and hymns, the local Methodist preacher probably spoke of the untimely death of the young English native struck down in the prime of life just as a promising future unfolded before him.

Mary was just ten months old.

Her mother, Jane, could neither read nor write. She instructed a neighboring farmer to prepare her late husband's gravestone. On the stone, the name "Rippon" is misspelled as "Rippin," perhaps an indication of how it was pronounced. Thomas's large, but thin, rectangular stone was typical of those in earlier cemeteries in New York and New England. On the front is a carving of a weeping willow tree, commonly used as a symbol of mourning. Underneath are the words:

MY HUSBAND
Sacred to the memory of
THOMAS F. RIPPIN
who died
March 27, 1851
age 31 years, 3 mos, 14 days

Mary was too young to remember her father when he died, but his death began a chain of events that also separated the young child from her mother.

CHAPTER 2

As a widow, Jane Rippon was suddenly at the mercy of the courts. Her father and a neighbor signed an affidavit stating that, to their knowledge, Thomas had not left a will. Illinois law specified that because her husband died intestate, most of his estate would not go to his widow, as it would today, but instead would be divided among his children. Since Mary was an only child, her guardianship records specified that her father's estate would be put in trust for her to inherit on her eighteenth birthday.

Jane, however, was allowed to live freely in the log cabin and was legally entitled to retain enough household items and provisions for one year.

Probate records in the Kendall County Circuit Court list the "Articles of specific property belonging to the estate of Thomas F. Rippon allowed by law to Jane, the widow of said Thomas Rippon." In the "Bill of Appraisement" they were itemized as follows:

> necessary beds, bedsteads, and bedding for herself and one child
> necessary household and kitchen furniture
> one spinning wheel
> one loom and its appendages
> one pair cards [for carding wool]
> one stove and the necessary pipe therefore
> wearing appcarcl [sic] for self and child
> one milk cow and calf
> one mare and colt
> one woman's saddle and bridle
> provisions for self and family for one year

four sheep
food for one horse
fuel for self and family, three months
other property allowed by statute

Within a few weeks of Thomas's death, Jane petitioned the court for the "other property." All were personal items that had belonged to her late husband. They were:

326 pounds of pork at four cents per pound
two pair boots
clock
one looking glass
one set of chairs
one rocking chair
three flat irons
two silk cravats
two cloth coats
one pair satinet pants
one velvet vest
lot crockery
twelve knives and forks

Jane was fortunate to have her parents and siblings nearby, but she chose not to depend upon their charity. Besides the personal items, she petitioned the court for an "allowance" of two hundred and twenty-four dollars—perhaps her late husband's savings—to be paid to her as separate property. In her affidavit, she explained her need by stating, "The said Thomas F. Rippon, deceased, left a Infant Child living with the undersigned." Jane signed with an *X*, legally binding as "her mark."

The late Thomas Rippon's real estate, his largest asset, was left untouched. He had increased his holdings to one hundred and sixty-six acres before his death.

State law required that all "infant heirs" have a guardian. Since Jane lacked any long-term ability to provide support, William Skinner Sr., Jane's father, was appointed Mary's legal guardian. A trust fund from the sale of some of the remainder of Thomas's personal property was set up to pay Mary's expenses. They included individual items such as doctor bills and clothing as well as child-support payments for her care. Since Mary lived with her mother, seventy-five dollars per year for "board" was paid to Jane.

The guardian's job was to manage Mary's funds in the best possible way to cover her needs. Income was raised by the continued sale of personal property such as fence posts and rails as well as by renting out pasture. The law did allow up to one-third of the "rents and profits" of the estate to go to Jane, but such payments were probably at the discretion of the guardian.

After a period of mourning, Jane was courted by Norman W. Whitney, an established farmer and landowner in the Lisbon Center community. They were married on September 1, 1853. Mary was three years old.

Norman Whitney sold his own property and moved in with Jane and Mary in the Rippon cabin. Mary's guardianship records show that he, as the new head of the household, received the seventy-five dollars annual stipend for her care. In return for farming her land, however, he was required to pay her account one hundred and thirty dollars per year. Unless contested, the farm belonged to Mary.

With Mary's grandfather's approval (as her guardian), funds were withdrawn from Mary's account to replace the log cabin with a permanent two-story frame home. Itemized receipts show nearly three hundred dollars' worth of expenditures for lumber, nails, window glass, lath, bricks, white paint, and numerous other building supplies. Carpentry fees include the laying and dressing of floors, the building of two flights of stairs, and the making of door and window frames. Mary's account even purchased fruit trees and provided timothy seeds for the cultivation of hay.

Mary's grandfather/guardian died when she was five years old. Her next guardian was her mother's brother William. Mary had several uncles living nearby, but William W. Skinner became her favorite. She mentioned him often in her diaries as an adult and affectionately called him "Uncle."

However, Uncle was not as accommodating as his father had been to Jane and Norman Whitney. As Mary's guardian, Uncle decided not only to provide for her ongoing care but to take legal steps to increase her inheritance.

In June 1856, when Mary was six years old, Jane exercised her "widow's right to dower." This was a legal action in which Jane filed a claim to one-third of the real estate owned by her daughter. According to the rules of the Illinois Revised Statutes, three "disinterested" commissioners were appointed by the Kendall County Circuit Court to survey the farm and legally "set off" Jane's portion "provided that the same can be made consistent with the interest of the estate."

Uncle saw this as his opportunity to intervene on Mary's behalf. In August 1856, Jane gave birth to Mary's half-brother. Since Jane was supported by her husband, Uncle was opposed to her claim on Mary's inheritance. A few weeks after the baby's birth, Uncle took Jane and her husband to court and filed his own "Petition for Dower."

In the case of "William Skinner, Guardian of Mary Ann Rippon vs. Jane Whitney and Norman Whitney," the Kendall County Circuit Court decreed that the farm could not be divided between mother and daughter "without manifest prejudice to the interests of other portions of said estate." The court determined that "It would be more advantageous to the interest of the said Mary Ann Rippon to have said premises sold and the monies arising from said sale put to interest, if the same could be sold for a fair price—and it also appearing by proof made in open court that the said real estate, together, is worth at least twenty-five dollars per acre."

Uncle had forced the sale of the Rippon farm and home. In October 1856, the Kendall County Circuit Court ordered the one hundred and sixty-six acres of the late Thomas Rippon's estate to be sold on the courthouse steps at public auction for Mary's "use and benefit." The requirements were one-fourth down in cash and the balance to be paid over ten years at ten percent interest per year.

The top bidders paid twenty-seven dollars and twenty-five cents per acre for a total of approximately four thousand dollars, more than one hundred forty-four thousand dollars in today's currency. The new owners took possession of the house and farm in November 1856. The Whitney family was without a home. Norman packed up Jane and the baby and moved to Kansas. Jane's six-year-old daughter, Mary, was left behind. The emotional toll on the child can only be imagined. Early in Mary's life it was apparent that among the adults, money was valued above family.

CHAPTER 3

AFTER THE FORCED SALE OF THE RIPPON FARM, UNCLE RELINQUISHED his role as Mary's guardian to neighbor and justice of the peace John Litsey. For two or three years, Mary lived with the Litseys on the Yorkville–Morris road across from Uncle's farm. Guardianship records reveal that the court paid the Litseys seventy-eight dollars per year for her "board."

The well-educated Litsey family was stimulating to the bright six-year-old. Before she had arrived, the Litseys had started the Lisbon Center school in their home. By the time Mary moved in, the community had erected its own building immediately south of the Litsey farm. This one-room frame school (torn down circa 1965) was painted white and was typical of its era. The classroom was twenty by thirty feet and entered through two cloakrooms, one for boys and one for girls. Two outhouses stood behind the building.

One teacher, usually a man, taught all eight grades. The teacher boarded in his students' homes, very likely including the Litseys. Everyone ate the usual diet of farm families: pork and potatoes, heavy bread, and biscuits. Considering the ample supply of pork (kept in a barrel) that Mary's mother had claimed as her own, it was a staple in their diet during Mary's early childhood too.

Classes were held from September to May. The day began at nine o'clock in the morning with the Pledge of Allegiance and a patriotic song. Often there was a prayer. Students participated in spelling bees and played baseball. They helped the teacher carry in corncobs and coal for the furnace and carry out the ashes. They also carried in buckets of water from the school's well. Everyone drank from the same dipper.

The school also served the community as a polling place and location for school board meetings. The building hosted programs and parties on holidays.

The families in the area worshipped at the Methodist Church, located on Lisbon Center Road west of Uncle's farm. At the time, in the late 1850s, the subject of slavery was constantly addressed in church lectures. The former New York residents had not forgotten their hatred of slavery and were likely to have discussed Harriet Beecher Stowe's new book, *Uncle Tom's Cabin*.

The Lisbon Center school straddled the property line between the Litsey farm and that of John Moore. He was a "station-keeper" on the Underground Railroad, harboring fugitive slaves who were passed from one home to another until they reached freedom in Canada. There was no actual railroad, but after many blacks were successfully smuggled out of the country, puzzled slaveholders compared their method of travel to a hypothetical underground railroad. The name stuck, and sympathizers adopted railroad terminology for their operations. Slaves were guided, usually at night, over fixed routes by "conductors" from one "station" or "depot" to another.

Harboring slaves was illegal, but county histories do not reveal any record of anyone in Lisbon Center having been caught or charged with the crime. Moore may have been just one of many in the community who adamantly believed in individual liberties. The example set to Mary and other neighborhood children was to do what they felt was right rather than what was expected by society.

In addition to absorbing lifelong values, Mary learned early about finances. As soon as she was old enough to understand, someone, likely John Litsey, taught her about the mortgage on her father's farm and the interest generated by its court-ordered sale. He likely explained that he and Uncle agreed on the need to increase her inheritance rather than just pay the bills. Litsey also may have explained to her how he, as guardian, loaned money from her account to John Moore and other farmers. When they paid it back at ten percent interest, it increased her principal. Mary's later account books show that she learned these lessons well.

When Mary was nine, she left the Litsey home and moved across the road to the Skinners, although Litsey remained her legal guardian. Mary's grandfather had willed his farm to Uncle, the oldest in the family. According to the 1860 federal census, household members included two other uncles and aunts, a baby, and a live-in "domestic."

Wherever the Skinners, Litseys, Moores, and the other neighbors gathered to socialize, whether it was at church, in the schoolhouse, or out in the fields, their anti-slavery sentiments reinforced their allegiance to the slave-free states of the North. The Lisbon Center community was overjoyed when fellow Illinois resident and prairie lawyer Abraham Lincoln was inaugurated as the sixteenth president of the United States in 1861. The residents followed newspaper accounts when, a few weeks into his presidency, the Confederates attacked Fort Sumter in South Carolina.

The day after the attack, President Lincoln called for seventy-five thousand volunteers to preserve the union. Within six days, the first of six Illinois regiments was mustered into service for a three-month term. Thousands of other young men who wanted to serve were turned away with the naive assurance that the rebellion would be over in sixty days.

By July 1861, most people realized that the war was far more serious than they initially were led to believe. The very existence of the whole country was threatened. They heeded Lincoln's own words when he said, "A house divided against itself cannot stand." Men from Kendall County formed the 36th Illinois Volunteers and prepared to leave for Missouri.

Although many left the county, the Civil War did not affect Mary's living arrangements, and she continued to reside in Uncle's home. In December 1861, when Uncle was thirty-two years old, he married seventeen-year-old Hannah Alford. Litsey, as justice of the peace, performed the marriage ceremony. Five months later, Hannah gave birth to their first son. Mary was eleven years old at the time. She and Hannah, whom she called "Auntie," formed a lifelong friendship.

As the war raged on and men continued enlisting, women replaced male teachers in the rural schools, giving Mary a glimpse of what it might look like to have a career of her own. Mary was thirteen when she completed her eight years of grammar school in 1863. At the time, no other schools existed in Lisbon Center, but the subject of continued education for girls was widely discussed in many women's magazines. The much-defined "woman's sphere" still placed a woman in the home, although several editorials stressed her need for further education in order to properly instruct her own children. Success was determined by how soon a woman got married, but society did acknowledge that should a woman become a widow or not marry, training was appropriate for a "useful occupation."

Most of Mary's classmates had dropped out along the way, or they chose not to go any further with their education, because they were needed at home to work in the fields or care for younger brothers and sisters. But with a trust fund to pay her expenses, Mary had more educational opportunities—and choices.

Chapter 4

Mary chose to study music in the town of Morris, ten miles south of Lisbon Center. The distance was too great to travel every day, so she boarded with another family. A receipt in her guardianship file shows six months of "tuition in music" from December 1863 to June 1864. The tuition cost forty dollars, while board for the same period cost sixty-five dollars. Grain wagons regularly rumbled back and forth between Lisbon Center and the larger town, so Mary likely returned to the Skinner farm on weekends.

One month into her lessons, John Litsey, as Mary's guardian, agreed to an extremely large purchase. Funds from her trust paid for a three-hundred-dollar piano. With the added expense of a piano cover and freight charges, the total was three hundred thirty-one dollars.

In today's currency, the piano would have cost nearly seven thousand dollars. The expense was greater than the construction of the updated Rippon house for which Mary's account had been charged.

The piano purchase is surprising not only for its cost but also because inflation had devalued the dollar by approximately one-fourth during the first three years of the Civil War. The piano was shipped from somewhere in the East through Chicago to Lisbon Center, either to the Skinner or Litsey home.

In 1865 at the close of the Civil War, Stillman Massey, a recent graduate of the University of Chicago and a veteran of the 134th Illinois Regiment, opened a private "select" school—the equivalent of today's high school—in the Morris Congregational Church. In an advertisement in the Morris newspaper at the time, Massey stated that particular attention would be given to students preparing for college and teaching positions. There is no proof that Mary attended, but because of a lifelong relationship with a friend named Miriam Barstow Massey, it is believed that she did.

Beginning in the fall of 1865, when Mary was fifteen years old, records show lump sums of money paid directly to her by Litsey. The payments ranged from fifteen to eighty-four dollars each. Some have no explanation, while others mention "tuition, board, and sundries." Mary in turn paid her own bills, whether they were for music lessons or high school.

After the Civil War, many single women who had replaced male teachers stayed on in the rural schools. The school boards approved because "the lady teachers," as they were called, did not have families to support and agreed to work for less pay. In *A History of Women's Education in the United States*, author Thomas Woody wrote that the female teachers could "use their position merely as a waiting station until the train came to bear them to their wedding." Rules in primary and secondary schools varied from district to district, but if a female teacher married, continuing to teach was "contrary to custom" and often forbidden.

To satisfy the demand for more teachers, publicly supported teacher-training schools, called normal schools, opened in various parts of the country. Their model, and namesake, was Illinois State Normal University (now Illinois State University), several hours southwest by train from Lisbon Center. The school had been founded in 1858 and contained a university and a high school in one building. In the fall of 1866, when Mary was sixteen, she entered the high school department. University students practiced their student teaching on Mary and her classmates. Again, as in Morris, Litsey relinquished money from her trust fund for Mary to pay her own tuition and living expenses.

Just as Mary began her first classes at the Normal School, she received word of the death of her thirty-nine-year-old mother. Mary and Jane had been separated for nine years, and it is not known if they corresponded or visited during that time. In Mary's personal journals from later years, the only mention of her mother was her date of death, September 8, 1866.

Meanwhile, thirty-seven-year-old Joseph Sewall, a teacher at Illinois State, took on a parental role for Mary. In later years, in various articles written about Mary, the Harvard-educated professor was reported to have been her chemistry teacher. However, records from Illinois State Normal University reveal that Sewall taught university courses rather than high school classes. It is possible that Mary took a college-level course, or that Sewall taught part of a high school class. Either way, they met while Mary was in high school, and he would greatly influence her career.

Before she graduated in June 1868, Mary received a letter of recommendation from her high school principal, William I. Pillsbury. It is evident that she was proud of the letter, as it has been carefully preserved. The principal wrote:

> This may certify that Miss Mary Rippon has been for more than a year a pupil in the high school department of the Normal School. During all this time she has had the respect and esteem of her teachers for her excellent deportment, her ladylike learning, and her scholarly habits. She has had much more than average success in her studies.

No records have survived to show if Mary applied to the school's university department. However, Illinois Normal required its university applicants to sign written commitments to teach in the Illinois school system for at least three years after graduation. Mary may not have wanted to be bound by a teaching agreement, as she was now of age and ready to receive her inheritance that would give her the freedom to do as she pleased.

CHAPTER 5

On May 25, 1868, Mary's eighteenth birthday, the Kendall County Circuit Court awarded her nearly three thousand five hundred dollars, equivalent to more than seventy-five-thousand dollars in current funds. Throughout the years, her former guardian, John Litsey, had made several loans and recovered them with interest. He also sold wheat harvested from Mary's fields. Even with his careful management, Mary's yearly living expenses, school tuition, the piano, and other expenses had cut into the balance of her father's estate. Mary still received a generous sum, although rapid inflation throughout the Civil War had cut her inheritance nearly in half.

Mary had become an heiress, but she had learned to manage her money and was not in a hurry to spend it. Her high school education had qualified her for a teaching position in a rural school, but she longed to continue her studies at Illinois Industrial University, now the University of Illinois, in Champaign. When she graduated from high school, however, Illinois Industrial University did not admit women.

Then, suddenly the world opened up to Mary in other ways. Possibly through a connection made by Sewall, Mary was introduced to Lucinda Stone of Detroit, Michigan. In Mary's diaries she always referred to her as "Mrs. L. N. Stone." The elder woman had made a name for herself as a "woman traveler" and was listed in Phebe A. Hanaford's 1882 book *Daughters of America, or Women of the Century.*

In 1871, when Mary was twenty-one, Mrs. Stone organized a "study group" of young women to learn about European art and civilization. The conclusion of the session was a chaperoned trip to Europe. Financially independent and on her own, Mary joined the group. Mrs. Stone was Mary's main—and perhaps only—female role model.

Mary was issued her first passport on June 20, 1871. At the end of their studies in Detroit, she and the other young women left the Midwest and boarded a train for the port city of New York. Mrs. Stone steered her young ladies through streets far busier than any they had seen in Chicago. Then they boarded a ship that carried them across the sea. Mary had never seen the ocean before, although Uncle may have told her stories of his family's voyage from England as a child.

In Germany, Mary met the von Brandis family, whose daughter Anna was Mary's age. The two became lifelong friends. Mary inquired about a university education and found that some of the European schools had somewhat more lenient policies in accepting women. Still, it took determination to fight the prejudices that existed against female scholars. Even twenty years later, at the University of Heidelberg, one female degree student was called "an upstart malcontent, as of no greater importance than a trained horse or seal."

When Mrs. Stone's tour was over, Mary remained with Anna in Germany and began a two-year course of study at the University of Hannover. Germany at the time was not only the first military power in Europe, it was also to the civilized world what Athens was to the Roman Empire. An 1885 article titled "University Education in Germany," in the University of Colorado archives, stated that Germany's "educational supremacy must excite the interest of all those nations whose sons and daughters are studying in her halls."

Back in America, readers hotly debated the new book *Sex in Education, A Fair Chance for Girls*, published in 1873. Author and physician Edward Clarke argued that to give women the same education as men was a "crime before God and humanity." He firmly believed that if a woman used her brain while menstruating, it would destroy her reproductive system! The education of women, he claimed, would lead to "race suicide," as the child-bearers of society would not be able to fulfill their duties.

Educated women were outraged. In 1874, several of them—along with a few men—published a collection of essays in a book of their own titled *Sex and Education, A Reply to Dr. E. H. Clarke's Sex in Education.* The writers encouraged women to pursue a college education. They were quick to point out that Clarke was an alarmist who based his theory on only seven of his patients rather than on scientific research. Feminist Julia Ward Howe, better known for writing "The Battle Hymn of the Republic," edited the reply and called Clarke's book "an intrusion into the sacred domain of womanly privacy."

In Europe, Mary followed her own very modern ambitions for further education. After becoming fluent in German, she decided to learn French and spent a year in Lausanne, a city in the French-speaking section of Switzerland. From there she took excursions into the Alps and acquired her appreciation for wildflowers. Her friend Anna lived with her in Lausanne through part of December 1874.

Before Anna left to return to Germany, Mary wrote a letter to Anna, but, for reasons known only to herself, she never mailed it. Instead, she placed it with her diaries, now in the University of Colorado archives, where it still remains today. The letter was written in French, in the flowery language common between women in the nineteenth century. Its contents are not conclusive but could connote a lesbian relationship. The references to "my precious little treasure" and "your husband" may have been Mary's synonyms for Anna and herself. Since relationships between young ladies and men were strictly chaperoned, it was not unusual for single women to develop emotional and sexual attachments with each other. Mary wrote:

> How I would like to be able to hold you tightly in my arms and to give you a thousand kisses. I would wish us a joyous Christmas and a happy [new] year, but when these two days will have arrived we will be quite far one from the other. I wouldn't have my precious little treasure, nor you your husband [*sic*]; but I will still be with you, if not in person, my heart and my thoughts will be there.
>
> You must not forget to send a thought about all of us, including me, who will be here all alone and having nobody with whom I would want to communicate my joys and my pain, but I shall have your letters which will give me the greatest pleasure. I know I still have you next to me, probably for the last time. I would like to keep you forever because

I know I will miss you so much. I cannot grasp the idea that it is tomorrow that you are leaving.

After Anna returned to Germany, Mary traveled to France, where she spent two years at the University of Paris. Nothing else is known of her life there at that time. No degree ever followed her name, and it is unlikely that she ever received one.

When Mary returned home, Auntie and Uncle had moved two counties south of Lisbon Center to a house in the town of Fairbury, in Livingston County, Illinois. While Mary was in Europe, she had missed the wedding of her friend Miriam Barstow and the "select" schoolteacher Stillman Massey. He had left the school to open a furniture store while his wife began teaching in a rural school.

For five years, Mary had soaked up European languages and cultures. She had explored cathedrals, art museums, and the architecture of medieval cities. The dusty roads of Fairbury and Lisbon Center must have seemed strangely unfamiliar, as if they belonged to another person or another lifetime. Mary, then twenty-seven, had broadened her view of the world far beyond the corn and wheat fields of her home state. The orphaned Illinois farm girl had become a world traveler and linguist. She was adept at handling her finances and living on her own.

Mrs. Stone arranged for Mary to become the German instructor at the high school in Detroit. After completing one year, Mary signed another year's contract for the 1877–1878 school year. Then, in August 1877, Mary received a letter from Joseph Sewall, the chemistry teacher whom she had met years before at Normal School. They may have kept up a correspondence while she was in Europe.

Sewall had been hired as the first president of the University of Colorado in Boulder. In September 1877, the university would open its doors for its first academic year. In his letter on August third, he wrote:

Miss Mary Rippon, Detroit Mich.

I am directed by the Board of Regents of the Colo. University to ask you to accept the position of teacher of French and German in the university, at a salary of twelve hundred dollars per year. I will add that for the first term you might be asked to teach some other branches but nothing to which you could object, I am sure. An immediate answer is required.

Respectfully, J. A. Sewall

PART 2
SINGLE YEARS, 1878–1887

CHAPTER 6

WHEN MARY RECEIVED JOSEPH SEWALL'S INVITATION, SHE HAD NEVER been west of Illinois. With her lengthy education and intense interest in European languages and cultures, she may not have given much thought to the expanding American frontier. The Great Plains extended all the way from the Midwest to the abruptly rising foothills that marked the eastern boundary of the Rocky Mountains. At the base of these foothills lay Joseph Sewall's new home in Boulder, Colorado.

In the fall of 1858, when Mary was eight, gold seekers had rushed to the Cherry Creek diggings near present-day Denver. A small party branched off from the group and headed north to the mouth of Boulder Canyon, then a part of Nebraska Territory. The men got out their gold pans, found some flakes, and continued to pan upstream in their search for the source of the gold. Others waited out the winter and built log cabins. The prospectors named their town Boulder City. When merchants arrived, Boulder City, shortened to Boulder, became a supply town for the miners.

Both Boulder County and Colorado Territory had been formed in 1861. During the Colorado Territorial legislature's first session, a Denver representative introduced a bill to establish a public university. At the time, Boulder had only three hundred residents, but their representative fought for the proposed university's location.

The town barely grew in the 1860s. Crude gold-processing mills, brought from the East, were unsuited to the recovery of Boulder County minerals. Many of the early prospectors left to try their luck elsewhere or moved to the plains and took up farming. Some signed up to fight in the Civil War. There were no reported Indian attacks in Boulder County, but Indian raids in eastern Colorado cut off early supply routes from the eastern states. Indian fighters from Boulder participated in conflicts that culminated in the Sand Creek Massacre in 1864. The public-university issue lay dormant.

In 1869, the discovery of silver in Caribou, high in the mountains near the Continental Divide, reinvigorated Boulder. Trade was increased between merchants and miners when farsighted entrepreneurs built a road up the previously inaccessible Boulder Canyon. A few years later, the discovery of tellurium in combination with gold and silver set off a second Boulder County gold rush.

Meanwhile, in 1872, territorial legislators debated moving the proposed location of the university to Denver, Colorado Springs, or Greeley. This prompted the immediate donation by three of Boulder's leading businessmen of fifty-two acres of land for a university site on a barren bluff just south of Boulder. The gift was a major step toward securing the university for Boulder, but funds were needed for a building. The small amount of money the townspeople could spare was going into bonds to bring in two competing railroads. The railroads' arrival, in 1873, lowered the shipping costs of Boulder County's mineral and agricultural products and aided in the area's economic development.

As Boulder evolved into a community of three thousand people, the problem of financing the proposed university remained. In 1874, fifteen thousand dollars were appropriated by the tenth Colorado Territorial Legislature on the condition that Boulder citizens match the funds. A year later, the residents reached their goal, hired an architect, and began construction of the University of Colorado's first building. While it was still under construction, President Ulysses S. Grant proclaimed Colorado the thirty-eighth state on August 1, 1876.

The University Building, as it initially was called, was completed in the spring of 1877, but a last-minute inspection by the regents revealed serious structural problems. The original slate roof was so heavy that cracks developed in the walls. Workmen removed the roof, added trusses, and replaced the slate with wood shingles. The damaged walls were reinforced with iron rods. The building was finally declared safe in July 1877, just two months before opening day.

Figure 6.1. When the University Building (Old Main) was under construction in 1876, it stood alone on a barren bluff south of the frontier town of Boulder, Colorado.
AUTHOR'S COLLECTION

When Mary received the letter from Joseph Sewall in August 1877, she had already made a commitment to teach high school in Detroit. Still, she replied with a request for more information. On October tenth, Sewall wrote her again.

Miss Mary Rippon, Detroit, Michigan

Your favor of the 1st received. The school "takes up" at nine a.m. Closes at two p.m. We have five recitations of about forty-five minutes each.

Probably you would not be required to teach more than three classes at first.

You would not have charge of an assembly room, but of a class or recitation room.

The teachers do not board in the building—tho, for the present we are living in the building. The town is about one half mile from the building. Best board—room, light, and fuel from $6 to $6.50 per week. We have now fifty-five pupils in attendance.

Very truly yours,

J. A. Sewall

The same month that Mary received Sewall's second letter, she read the October 1877 issue of *Atlantic Monthly*. Later she told an interviewer that she had been greatly influenced by Helen Hunt Jackson's article, "The Procession of Flowers in Colorado." Jackson, an Easterner who had reluctantly moved to Colorado for health reasons, wrote of the beauties of Colorado's wildflowers.

Editor Amos Bixby of the *Boulder County News* commented on Sewall's first month as university president. In the same month as Helen Hunt Jackson's article, Bixby wrote:

> There is none of the musty, slow book-worm about Dr. [*sic*] Sewall. He is an active, enthusiastic, practical worker in the school room and in the world. Upon the rostrum his is a power, for he speaks with elegance, force, and remarkable purity . . . He is temperate in all his habits, using neither tobacco nor liquor.

During the time Mary was teaching in Detroit and corresponding with Sewall, she attended a Congregational Church conference and met a minister who had recently returned from Boulder. He explained the structural problems of the University Building and tried to talk her out of considering a move to Boulder. The minister emphasized the university's isolation from the small town, and he warned her that the three-story brick structure could easily blow over in Boulder's strong winds.

Undaunted, and against the advice of her friends, Mary decided to accept Sewall's offer. She found another teacher to take over her contract in Michigan. Sewall wrote her again in December, confirming that she would start at the beginning of the second term in January of

1878. According to the regents, her salary would be twelve hundred dollars per year, "as low a salary as a competent teacher can be procured for." It was equivalent to nearly thirty-seven thousand dollars today.

Sewall also emphasized that a banker had given the university two thousand dollars, a sizable sum with which to start a library. The cash donation for books reassured Mary that she had made the right decision. A few weeks before she was to start, Mary wrote to Sewall and formally accepted his offer.

In early January 1878, Mary boarded a train in Detroit, then transferred to another in Chicago. She watched as the familiar farmlands of her childhood transformed into undulating prairie and then a nearly barren landscape punctuated with strange rock formations. Two and a half days later, she reached Cheyenne. There, in Wyoming Territory, she got off the large through-train and climbed into the pullman coach on the small Colorado Central. A steam engine, two coaches, and a pullman sleeper made up the entire train. Just a few months earlier, travelers had bumped and swayed in a cloud of dust on the Wells Fargo stagecoach line. On the new local train, Mary and the other passengers sat on rich Brussels upholstery surrounded by mahogany paneling. Polished brass kerosene lamps hung overhead.

On the route south from Cheyenne, the train remained on the plains but paralleled the eastern edge of a series of north–south mountain ranges. Visible in the fading daylight was Longs Peak, the lofty sentinel of the Front Range.

As the train approached Boulder, neatly kept houses and barns were set like checkers in a patchwork quilt of fenced-in farms. Huge rock slabs in the foothills loomed in front of layers and layers of jagged mountains that seemed to go on forever in the distance.

On January 5, 1878, a few minutes before six o'clock in the evening, Mary stepped off the train at the small frame Colorado Central depot a mile or two east of Boulder. Years later, in a newspaper interview, she spoke of the evening she arrived and recalled, "I was almost alone in the Pullman when the train stopped. Dr. Sewall was there to meet me. The daylight had faded but a new moon cast enough light to show up the

Figure 6.2. Joseph Sewall had left his teaching position at the Illinois State Normal School (where Mary had attended high school) to become the first president of the University of Colorado.

wonderful line of the snowclad mountains. The air was that of a perfect January evening, clear, dry, and bracing."

As the story goes, one of the first questions Sewall asked was, "How does it look to you?" Mary was said to have replied that it reminded her of the Alps; that it was "glorious." Sewall replied, "Well, my spirits have risen a hundred per cent. My wife told me you would not stay two days in this lonely place."

A sixteen-passenger omnibus, its sides decorated with colored oil paintings of Boulder Canyon scenes, soon pulled up to the depot. As trunks were loaded on top, four white horses stomped impatiently to be off. Their condensed breath hung like a cloud around their heads in the cold night air.

Mary's first view of Boulder's homes and businesses was from the omnibus as it stopped to let passengers off at each of the town's three hotels. Sewall had reserved a room for her at the American House, the hotel nearest the university. He made sure she was settled, then bid her goodnight and promised to send his oldest daughter, Addie, in the morning.

CHAPTER 7

THE DAY AFTER MARY'S ARRIVAL WAS A SUNDAY. AS THE SUN ROSE boldly over the eastern horizon, the rocky face of the mountains to the west changed from a pre-dawn gray to a soft glowing pink. The flat outcroppings that Mary had seen from the train the previous night had gained a third dimension and revealed various shades of reds and browns. In contrast were the snow-covered bushes and evergreen trees that clung to the steep inclines behind them.

Eighteen-year-old Addie Sewall met Mary at her hotel. The daughter of the university president offered to take the new instructor to church and to show her the University Building. They walked through the parlor of the American House, elegantly furnished with a marble center table, mirrors, and a piano. In the reading room were Mark Twain novels, a few English classics, and current copies of the *Boulder County News* and the *Colorado Banner*. The hotel was comfortable, but seven dollars per week for room and board would take up more than a quarter of Mary's salary.

The two women wrapped themselves tightly in their woolen cloaks and stepped into the thin but bracing air. They walked from the hotel, at Fourteenth and Front (now Walnut) Streets, past the town square to the First Congregational Church on Pine Street. The church bell, in its modest brick tower, announced the beginning of services.

Mary and Addie climbed the short winding staircase to the sanctuary. Most of the ladies were seated, but several men warmed their hands near the two big pot-bellied stoves on either side of the room. The glow from a few kerosene lamps filled the shadows missed by the sunlight as it shone through the plain glass windows. Wooden benches were covered with deep red cushions.

Figure 7.1. Services at the original building of Boulder's First Congregational Church were well-attended.
CARNEGIE LIBRARY FOR LOCAL HISTORY/MUSEUM OF BOULDER COLLECTION

If Mary expected to be isolated from the amenities of civilization, she was in for a surprise. The hymns were familiar, and the people refined. After the service, Mary and Addie walked along the wooden sidewalks of Pearl Street, where shopkeepers had attempted to shovel off the latest snow. Bradley & McClure, Boulder's largest dry goods store, was on the north side of Pearl Street. A placard in the nearby window of Geo. C. Squires Boots and Shoes advertised "ladies' boots expressly for wear on our rocky soil."

The women had to keep moving to keep their feet warm. On the way to the University Building, they crossed the wooden Twelfth Street (now Broadway) bridge over Boulder Creek and looked down as the water trickled under the clumps of ice that had formed along its banks. Beyond the bridge, there were no sidewalks, so they lifted their long skirts a few inches off the ground and walked in the wagon tracks on the road. Finally, they reached the bluff south of the town.

At the top of the hill, the women lifted their skirts again and climbed over a homemade stile in a cattle fence. There was no handrail. According to an early visitor, the stile consisted of a plank nailed on top of a barrel cut in half, another plank that was laid across two whole barrels, and, on the other side, a third plank on two more half barrels. Addie explained that the stile was needed to keep the Sewalls' cow within the fence and all other livestock out.

The only path to the university led over a high, rough, rickety bridge across a small ravine. The imposing three-story brick University Building stood alone on the barren plain without even a bush or a tree nearby. From its front entrance, the building looked down on the small city of Boulder. The building was Addie's home and all that existed of the University of Colorado.

The women climbed the steep stone steps, pulled open the heavy front door, and were greeted by Joseph's Sewall's wife, Anne. She had been waiting for them in her sitting room, off the hall on the right. Mary met the Sewalls' new baby and was reacquainted with Addie's brother and two younger sisters. The family's living quarters were homey and comfortable; they even included indoor plumbing. As long as the janitor stoked the coal furnace in the basement, the rest of the building was warm. The only exception, Mary was told, was during strong winds when the family huddled around a small Franklin stove.

As the first day of the second term would begin the next morning, Mary had only this one day to learn her way around. Joseph Sewall came in and showed Mary his office and the unfinished assembly hall with its twenty-nine-foot ceiling. They walked through three recitation rooms, but only one on the first floor was furnished with desks and blackboards.

A long flight of stairs led from the main vestibule to the second floor. Two other stairways were located at the west and south entrances. Six additional classrooms were upstairs. One in the northwest corner of the building was ready for students.

The library faced the mountains from a sunny room in the southwest corner of the second floor. Newspaper editor Amos Bixby, who often reported on the state of affairs at the university, praised the indispensable selection of new books and added, "It is hard to tell which is the most pleasing to beauty-loving eyes, the sandstone and ever-green colors of the confronting mountains or the combination of the rich, dark brown colors in the Brussels carpet covering the library room floor."

The flight of stairs on the west side of the building led to the third floor where there were eleven student-study rooms and sleeping quarters for the few out-of-town students.

The janitor and his family had rooms in the basement. Also in the basement were the kitchen, dining room, music department, furnace room, and space to display mineral specimens and assay equipment. Sewall continued to teach chemistry, and during this first year he had a small chemical laboratory in the basement—but the fumes were not appreciated upstairs.

In Sewall's opening day oration, he had stated that although the building and the plans for the university were impressive, they were mere "trappings" and cautioned against judging them any more than judging a man on his form. "The real test of the university," he said, "like that of man, would be its character." Sewall spoke of "honor, fidelity, and stainless integrity" and emphasized "what we do is what we are."

One Sunday evening, shortly after Mary's arrival in Boulder, Sewall gave one of his popular orations in the Congregational Church. Bixby reported that even though the university president had not studied theology, he "spoke with a sharp, crisp, honest, manly expression which everyone could appreciate and understand."

As expected, Sewall spoke on education, but connected it with Biblical morality. He indicated his message in his introductory comments, saying, "The demand of the age is men of lofty moral purity and broad mental culture. To have the first without the second or the second without the first should be a bar to high and holy trust as an educator."

Sewall stressed human responsibility and what he called "its inevitable high or low destiny." He concluded by nearly shouting, "Let young men and young ladies come to the university. We guarantee their safety in morals and advancement in learning!"

To keep her new position, Mary would have to live up to her employer's expectations and, as it developed, keep a great part of her life a secret.

CHAPTER 8

ON HER FIRST DAY OF TEACHING, MARY AGAIN CLIMBED THE HILL, went up and over the stile in the cattle fence, and crossed the bridge over the ravine. A January thaw brought relief from the bitter cold but made the snow sloppy and slushy. Clumps of snow slipped off the pines and firs and gave the mountains a darkened hue.

The janitor rang the bell announcing the nine o'clock chapel service. A crowd had gathered in the unfinished assembly hall. Joseph Sewall introduced Mary to Professor Justin Dow, a heavyset former high school teacher who taught Latin and Greek. Sewall taught history, geography, and the sciences in addition to fulfilling his duties as president.

Conversations ceased immediately when Sewall rose to speak. The *Boulder County News* reported that he welcomed everyone in the room to the second term, read a verse from the Scriptures, led the hymn "A Mighty Fortress Is Our God," then ended with the Lord's Prayer. He introduced "Miss Rippon" and explained that she had been hired to teach modern languages but had agreed, at least for the current term, to teach English grammar and mathematics as well.

Except for some interior carpentry, the building was finished, and Sewall and his staff of two were prepared. All that was needed were qualified students. The very first high school graduating class in the entire new state of Colorado had been in Boulder the previous year, but even those students had not been prepared to take a university entrance exam.

For the new school year, thirty-eight young men, twenty-seven young women, and their teacher, Justin Dow, had been moved to the university from Boulder's overcrowded Central School. Fifty of these students were in the high school preparatory department, still completing the requirements to enter the first university class. The rest were enrolled in teacher-training classes in the normal department. There were no university-level students at all.

The Boulder community was curious about its new lady instructor. Mary dressed modestly in the latest fashions made by her dressmaker in Detroit. On her passport application, she had described herself as "five feet six inches tall with a high forehead, gray eyes, long nose, small mouth, short chin, light-brown hair, light complexion, and an oval face." One of her students later described her as "a quiet, low-voiced, attractive young woman full of efficient energy and wholly devoted to her work."

Within the first two weeks of classes, Mary was visited in the classroom by on-the-scene editor Amos Bixby of the *Boulder County News* along with Boulder Regent L. W. Dolloff. Both men said they were impressed with the thoroughness of her teaching and her five years of study abroad. The academic level was no different from that at which she had taught in Detroit.

As the crisp days of winter softened into spring, Mary left her classroom from time to time to begin her search for wildflowers. When the summer sun grew intense on the plains, Mary joined the Sewalls for family picnics in the canyons in the foothills. By the fall of 1878, after the lavender asters and the piercing blue columbines in the mountains had faded, ten preparatory students had been recruited to become the university's first freshman class. Both men and women were welcome.

Bixby had already reported the university's philosophy that stated, "Western colleges do not have to follow slavishly eastern examples. Men and women alike should have equal access to all state institutions of higher learning and a voice in determining the nature of the curriculum." By then, the Universities of Minnesota, Nebraska, Michigan, and Wisconsin had joined Utah, Iowa, and Kansas in coeducation.

"At the same time," Bixby continued, "a major purpose of the University would be to produce responsible citizens, and, to that end, some commonly accepted morality should also be taught, along with the social graces to enable University graduates to function as civilized people."

Students and faculty were enthusiastic about the beginning of the new term. The *Boulder News and Courier* stated that the teachers, including Mary, were "fresh and hopeful." Their outlook was so full of promise "that Heaven and Earth seemed to smile on the young institution and wish it Godspeed."

For the first time in her teaching career, Mary found herself teaching university students, although they were the same young men and women she had taught in the preparatory department the preceding year. Only the course material had changed. No longer did she have to teach mathematics and English grammar. Finally, she could devote all of her time in the classroom to French and German language and literature. Every morning, she wrote a list of questions and answers on the blackboard. Students responded with both oral recitations and written examinations.

From time to time, observers sat in on Mary's classes and evaluated her work. After she had taught for two years, a visiting German literature professor from the University of New York reported that, "Miss M. Rippon has done praiseworthy work, as her classes proved, in teaching the French and German languages. It remains only to remark that the zeal and tact she displays in her vocation deserve unrestricted acknowledgment."

When Max Herman was in office as a regent in the early 1880s, he praised her by stating, "In this department Miss Rippon presides, a lady who not content with learning the languages from textbooks exclusively, took up her residence at the very fountains from which they spring, learning German at Hannover and French at Paris. Her pronunciation is purer than that of many Frenchmen and Germans and is absolutely perfect in both branches."

But perhaps not everything had gone smoothly for Mary. There must have been some criticism of her teaching methods, as Herman then defended her by saying, "Let us hear no more about imperfection in the teaching of these branches. Such things must emanate from the ignorant or be the offsprings of minds biased and opinionated beyond all sense."

Mary's individual attention and gentle teaching style made her quite popular not only with her colleagues but also with her students. Their loyalty helped when her position was challenged by a German man, C. von Trotha, who threatened her job. Years later, Timothy Stanton, one of the students at the time, explained that von Trotha felt that he, rather than Mary, was better qualified to teach German.

Stanton related, "The fact that a rigorous, if insidious, campaign was being carried on to displace the beloved Miss Rippon soon became known to the students, and they proposed to make their objections known in the most vigorous manner they could think of. So, one evening, all the male students met downtown on Pearl Street with all the noise-making instruments that were available and awaited the cover of darkness for a call on the would-be professor."

Sewall heard of the march just as it was about to start. He sent word to the student leaders that the proposed demonstration would not help, and he promised that if the students would give it up, he would treat them to an oyster supper. Stated Stanton, "That was all that was needed to crush the rebellion, and soon the students were seated with their president in the dining room in the basement of the University Building." The Board of Regents then issued its own statement saying that no vacancy existed for the chair of modern languages.

Mary was dealing now with the male world of academia. At the time, professional women educators were practically unknown. A few private eastern women's schools, such as Smith and Wellesley, had women professors, but they only taught other women. Mary had both men and women in the university classroom.

As stated in the university's philosophy, Sewall placed education and morality on the same plane. As one of few female professors, how Mary lived her life—and the example she set for her students—would be as important as the subjects she taught them in the classroom.

Chapter 9

For several years, Mary's life fit Joseph Sewall's standards. Promotions and freedom unknown to most single women of her time followed Mary's growing respect and popularity. In the spring of 1881, after the university was declared "in a flourishing condition," the regents elevated Mary's status from an instructor to full professor and named her the chair of the modern language department. Her salary was raised from twelve hundred to fourteen hundred dollars per year, equivalent in today's currency to more than forty-two thousand dollars.

Even with the raise, however, Mary's salary was not equal to that of her male colleagues. Fellow professors at the time received an annual salary of two thousand dollars. Additional male professors were added throughout the years, and all were consistently paid more than Mary. The rationalization was the same as that of the rural school boards who hired female schoolteachers after the Civil War. Male teachers were expected to support wives and children, so their higher pay was considered appropriate. Single women had no dependents and could live on a lower salary.

Teaching at any level was considered a temporary position for a woman until her marriage. Even at Boulder's Central School, parents and students joked about "matrimonial fever" and how it caused a turnover of the lady teachers. A woman's mission in life was to care for and nurture her family. According to *A Woman's Proper Place: A History of Changing Ideals and Practices 1870 to the Present*, the job of unmarried women, in Mary's time, was to "purify and amend society."

If Mary thought her salary unfair, she never filed a complaint. Instead, she savored the freedom of managing her money as she wished instead of turning it over to a husband. Teaching was her career, her life's work. In a society in which gender dictated male and female "spheres," Mary's professional goals had gravitated toward those of men.

Mary also enjoyed the freedom to come and go as she pleased. In the summer of 1880, when she was thirty, the *University Portfolio* reported that she and Addie Sewall took the train and visited family and friends in Illinois and Michigan. Now, instead of needing a chaperone, Mary had become one. The trip included a stop at Uncle and Auntie's new home in the town of Fairbury, Illinois.

Each year, when the first anemones bloomed in the spring, Mary rented a horse and sidesaddle and alone explored the canyons along the edge of the mountains. The wildflowers had become her favorite, and her diary entries often included comments such as, "Out gathering anemones last Saturday. Succeeded in finding many very pretty ones." The entire bluff south of Boulder was open country except for the University Building and its fenced-in cow, the small Pioneer (also called Columbia) Cemetery, and one or two ranches where cattle ranged freely and munched on wild yucca blossoms.

Sewall attempted to landscape the still-barren university campus. A few scraggly trees had been planted around the big brick building, but as the first graduation approached in 1882, a crew of workmen used horse-drawn dump wagons to haul in topsoil. The first load blew away, and they had to do it all over again.

Sewall, his wife, Anne, and Mary planted grass, lilacs, and a circle of apple trees to the east of the building. Mary also planted wild plums, that grew into a thicket along the ravine. The workmen set out more than one hundred maples and elms. As sizable rocks were uncovered, the men moved them to the lower end of the ravine and started building a dike for a pond.

Gradually the university began to look more settled, and the University Building became known as Old Main. In June 1882, the assembly hall was decorated for its first graduation ceremony. Six of the initial ten students made up the first graduating class.

Framed photographs of the graduates—all men—hung over a rostrum beneath evergreen boughs formed into the letters of their surnames. The graduates gave lengthy orations that were followed by Sewall's

Figure 9.1. Mary posed for this portrait on a visit to Illinois in 1882.
CARNEGIE LIBRARY FOR LOCAL HISTORY/MUSEUM OF BOULDER COLLECTION

eloquent commencement address. He had already tied together his favorite topics of education and religion by giving a Baccalaureate sermon. His text, from the Bible's Book of Proverbs 4:7, was "Wisdom is the principal thing, therefore, get wisdom, and with all thy getting, get understanding."

Anonymously, the graduates published their "personal characteristics of the senior class." Their average age was twenty-three. Four of the men planned to become lawyers, one was undecided between law and journalism, and one planned to teach. On the topic of hair, the men wrote, "Three of us wear burnsides, from the bushy, vain-glorious type to the sickly, faintly don't look at me, please, kind. One bangs his hair, one has been caught in curl papers, four caress mustaches, and one wears a smooth face." None of the graduates claimed to swear. Three smoked and the majority were "strong temperance men." On religion they stated, "One is a Congregationalist, one a Methodist, one a Unitarian, one is undecided, one professes to believe in the Koran, and one has no religion."

Additionally, "Two [of the men] would vote for 'women's rights,' meaning the suffrage, one would not, one is for woman's rights—rights to manage the household, while two are lukewarm as to the whole question. One is decidedly against co-education and five are for it."

> In a section on amusements, the graduates wrote,
> Oh, a starry night for a ramble
> In a flowery dell,
> Neath the bush and bramble,
> Kiss, and never tell.

* * *

A few months later, in her usual brief and factual diary, Mary slipped in a single entry, which read, "very lonely."

CHAPTER 10

BEFORE LONG, SEVERAL NEW FACULTY MEMBERS, ALL MEN, HAD BEEN hired by the university. Winthrop Scarritt, a preparatory department instructor, was most attentive to Mary. She had moved out of the hotel into a boarding house where "Mr. Scarritt," as she called him, came to play cards. He was from Indiana and had also grown up on a midwestern farm.

When the anemones were in bloom again, Mary searched as usual on horseback. Before one of her rides, Scarritt asked if he could accompany her. Throughout the spring of 1883, Mary and her male companion rode together several times. At least once they went to Boulder Falls, in Boulder Canyon, and another time they rode partway up Left Hand Canyon. Occasionally, after they returned to Boulder, he took her to one of the hotels for dinner.

Whatever Scarritt's attentions, Mary confided in her diary that she would not allow him to pursue her. Instead, she asked the regents for a sabbatical leave in order to further her studies abroad. In June 1883, after the end of the school year, she moved out of her boarding house and stored most of her belongings in a private home. Scarritt saw her off at the depot. It is remarkable that she had been able to save for such a trip on her meager salary.

The train ride between Boulder and Illinois had become familiar to Mary. When she got off the train at Fairbury, humidity hung above endless fields of green. Uncle met her at the depot and took her to see Auntie and the boys for a few days. After she boarded the train again, she stopped in Chicago and spent one hundred dollars—almost a month's salary—on her steamer ticket. She renewed friendships in Detroit and picked up new dresses she had ordered from her faithful seamstress who "sewed all day" for her.

One of Mary's former students, Helen Coleman, also planned a yearlong trip to Europe and needed a chaperone. Her family probably offered Mary a small fee as a companion and tutor. Mary met her student in New York City, where they shopped at Macy's Department store and walked the newly completed Brooklyn Bridge, then boarded their steamship, the *Elbe*.

The first two days were smooth, but on the third, the sea began to get rough. Passengers were ordered to stay inside. Huge waves swept across the upper deck and soaked everything in sight. As the ship lurched from the crest of one wave to another, Mary noted in her diary, "Sick all day and did not leave my room. Rainy and cold."

A few days later she wrote, "Better. Sat in ladies' salon nearly all day. Talked with Mrs. Wilson of Philadelphia." The next day's entry was "Rainy, evening fine. Dancing, illumination." Like a glowing palace in the middle of nowhere, the *Elbe* was brilliantly lit with electric lights powered by a generator that ran off the ship's steam engine. As the passengers gathered in the lounge or on deck, they pulled out their maps and discussed their prospective trips. At dusk, they enjoyed the changing colors of the sunset and occasionally spotted whales and other wildlife. They knew they were close to land when a flock of birds followed their ship.

As soon as they could see land, many of the passengers watched the shoreline with excitement. Soon they picked out fields, houses, and even a moving train. After a stop at Southampton, they continued through the English Channel where lighthouses from both Dover, England, and Calais, France, brightened the darkening waters. Finally, after a night in the North Sea, Mary and Helen ate their last shipboard breakfast, docked at Bremerhaven, Germany, and boarded a train to Hannover.

Mary found a boarding house for Helen, then immediately looked up her old friend Anna. She, too, had remained unmarried, although the rest of her life remains a mystery. Nine years had passed since they had parted as friends, and perhaps lovers, in Lausanne, Switzerland. Mary wrote in her diary that Anna was "just as lovable as ever." With her, Mary could just be herself. Or maybe it was a self that she wanted to try out for a while. She confided to her diary that the two women "smoked cigarettes." Another time they "drank champagne." Uncle, Joseph Sewall, and her students would have been shocked. Obviously, Helen was not with them at the time. Unlike in Boulder, Mary was not under any pressure here to be anyone's role model.

There was plenty for Mary and Anna to do in Hannover. They went sightseeing and shopping, as carefree as schoolgirls. Mary bought an album to start a new collection of pressed wildflowers and wrote that the chocolates were "excellent." One evening they attended a performance of Franz Lizt's *Faust Symphony* that Mary noted was "beautiful beyond description." In Boulder, she had taught Johann Wolfgang von Goethe's treatment of the Faust drama to her students. Faust risked self-destruction when he made a pact with Mephistopheles (the Devil) in his lifelong search for knowledge, power, and youth. Mary had engaged her students in long classroom discussions about transcending human limitations in one's quest for self-realization.

Anna was left behind when Mary resumed her responsibilities to Helen. Professor and student immersed themselves in German culture through a study of its religion and art. Mary took Helen to various places of worship, including a Jewish synagogue and services in several Protestant churches. Mary and Helen also attended Mass in a Catholic cathedral, where they were surprised to see the king and queen of Saxony. For days they walked through art museums. They traveled by train to Berlin, Dresden, Nuremberg, and Munich, where Mary continued to teach her student about German culture.

Back on the train again, the women traveled to Verona, Venice, Florence, and Rome. They attended Mass at St. Peter's Basilica and wandered around the Vatican, admiring the sculptures. Mary was particularly impressed with Italy and may at that time have begun to feel a need to share its art and culture with other women.

Her underlying restlessness may have been stimulated by the fragrant flowers and warm evenings. In a speculative moment, Mary entered into her diary, "Tried to decide future plans and failed."

Mary and Helen returned to Hannover, where Anna took over Helen's education. Mary went alone to study art in Paris. A few months later, she was visited by Ernest Pease, one of her former students. In a letter home to his fiancée, Ernest wrote,

> It did seem such a treat to see her, and I doubt if she can remember of ever having such a "squeezing" before. It was after nine before I found her, but we did some lively talking that evening I assure you . . . It does seem so strange that we should meet abroad and in Paris too. It is more like a dream. In college I used to enjoy listening to her descriptions of Europe so much, and Addie [Sewall] and I were always full of questions.

Ernest was in Paris to research a manuscript at the Bibliotheque Nationale but spent part of every afternoon at the Louvre Museum with Mary. She still delighted in giving him individual attention. In Ernest's next letter, he wrote, "She is splendid to show me about for she is familiar with all the artists and their works and so points out to me the beauties." In yet another letter he added, "Miss Rippon has this winter been studying the originals [paintings] so each picture was like meeting an acquaintance whom she introduced to me."

After Ernest's visit was over, Mary took a steamer to London and, as usual, was quite seasick. In London, she met up again with Helen who had just come from Anna's. In 1884, more than a year after Mary and Helen had left New York, they sailed back on the S.S. *Austral*, a steamship of the Orient Line. Mary briefly continued her diary, noting another bout of seasickness. She also commented on "several disagreeable children" on board.

Eight days later, the ship docked in New York. United States immigration authorities required all four hundred and eighty-one passengers to be listed before they disembarked. Even though it conflicted with her passport, the ship's passenger list gave Mary's age as thirty when she really was thirty-four.

Chapter 11

Mary arrived back in Boulder in time for the 1884 fall semester. Before long, she fell back into her teaching routine and became involved with the community. She took her belongings out of storage and moved into a private home, an option that was more economical than the hotel and more private than the boarding house.

Others had moved around, too. The state legislators had provided a fund for additional university buildings, and the Sewalls were finally able to live in an official house of the president. Their new and elegant brick home gave Joseph Sewall and his family room to expand and entertain. The Sewalls' old living quarters were refurnished as additional classrooms in Old Main. Although most of the students were still from the Boulder area and lived at home, two new brick cottages accommodated out-of-town students. One was for men, and one was for women.

Sometimes Mary stayed overnight with the young ladies. She enjoyed their company, but each year their age gap increased. She listened to the students' problems and concerns with the responsibility of a dean of women even though there was no such position at the university at the time. Except for a housemother, Mary was their only other female authority figure.

Winthrop Scarritt, who had corresponded with Mary throughout the year she was overseas, had left his position and moved away. The state's budget for higher education was strained by the School of Mines in Golden and the new Agricultural College (now Colorado State University) in Fort Collins. Even so, the University of Colorado in Boulder hired new faculty members.

Canadian-born Dr. James Washington Bell had substituted in Mary's French and German classes while she was on sabbatical. When she returned, Dr. Bell was able to resume his own interests, and he chaired the department of political economy and history. Dr. Bell and his wife, Delphine, had lived in Germany where he received his doctoral degree. Shortly afterward, he developed a hemorrhage in one of his lungs. His physician had advised a change of climate that took the family first to Switzerland and then to Boulder. Professor J. Raymond Brackett also joined the faculty and taught English literature and Greek. His recent bride, Lottie, remained behind in Maine until she gave birth to their son, William. Then she and the baby joined her husband in Boulder.

Mary soon found she had a lot in common intellectually with the two new professors and their wives. Even though she was single, and Lottie and Delphine were occupied with caring for their young children, the couples welcomed her company. Mary, the Bracketts, and the Bells became lifelong friends.

The growth of the university and its new faculty spurred both an intellectual and a spiritual movement in Boulder. At the movement's center was the Unitarian Church, which had been established in Boulder while Mary was overseas. Sewall had joined with two of his daughters, Addie and Jennie. Jennie (who later wrote the memoir *Jane, Dear Child*) quoted her father as stating, in reference to the Unitarians, "I'm glad to say there's a group of liberals." Their minister had stated that "Unitarianism had stood for something in this community, and that there was a need in Boulder for a liberal society." The minister also had a romantic interest in Addie.

Several of Mary's university colleagues started a Unitarian Literary Union that was open to men and women and centered on reading and discussion of literature. The programs, called "Dime Sociables," provided an income for the church and were held once a month in the evenings. Mary usually attended. One evening when she did not, she wrote in her diary, "Was tired. Weather cold. Made good fire and stayed at home feeling uncomfortable about Unit. [Unitarian] sociable."

Mary's friendships with the professors' wives grew. As she reflected on what she had learned abroad, she discussed the subject of women's clubs with two other interested women. They agreed to invite eight other women to another meeting in Mary's rented room, on the corner of Fourteenth and Front (now Walnut) streets.

After that initial meeting, a larger group of women met to organize what was first known as the Ladies' Literary Club. Delphine Bell and Mary were elected as officers. Soon the club evolved into the Boulder Fortnightly Club. Members were carefully selected and the number limited. The *Denver Sunday Times* explained, "The key which opens the door of initiation into the [Boulder] Fortnightly must be stamped 'Superior Intellect.' From each member is required intellectual work, and commonly speaking, there are no places for drones."

Because Mary was so enthusiastic about her recent trip, she chose the topic of the history and art of Florence, Italy, for the next meeting. She also shared with the members her collection of art reproduction prints from the National Museum in Florence. A newspaper reporter stated:

> This club promises to be a pleasant thing for the ladies of the university town. It brings together many who being relieved of household and daily cares for a few hours can find recreation in listening to the thoughts and experiences of others. Of course, all could read at home the books selected, but to read in company with others and especially with several who have traveled through Italy and can tell much of the Florentine people from acquaintance will make the works much more interesting.

The club helped Mary broaden her female friendships beyond student, church, and university connections. All but one other woman and Mary were married. Of one of these married members, Mary wrote, "She read while washing dishes, she churned with one hand and held a book with the other, her deft fingers knitted rapidly while her eyes and thoughts were on the printed page."

Emma Wangelin, another married member, also reflected on the early Fortnightly meetings. In a letter to Mary years later, she wrote:

> I remember I felt very much honored at being asked to the first meeting and the ladies I met there charmed me. My life at that time was

so taken up with tending babies (I had three little ones then and had laid away another) that I had little time to give to literary pursuits, but when Fortnightly was started, I rejoiced at the privilege of attending and listening to papers, talks, readings, and discussions on topics other than domestic or maternal ones. Many a time did my husband desert his desk in the office and come home for two hours to take care of the babies so I could attend the meetings of the Club. He said I came back so refreshed that he felt repaid.

The Unitarians eventually disbanded when the minister joined a Denver church and took Addie Sewall as his bride. Mary returned to, but never formally joined, the Congregational Church she had attended when she first arrived in Boulder. She stayed active in the Boulder Fortnightly Club, enjoying the company of other women.

By the end of the spring semester of 1885, delicate fragrant blossoms had formed on the plum trees that Mary had planted west of the dammed-up ravine. Outside Old Main, saplings began to mature into young trees. The university had started to look settled, but underneath, the institution was plagued with unsettling financial woes.

CHAPTER 12

As the communities of Boulder, Golden, and Fort Collins competed for economic development, their universities competed with each other for funds. All three were dependent upon the state legislators, yet a majority of those legislators questioned the need for higher education at a time when the new state was about to embark on the building of its capitol in Denver. In 1885, financial requests from all three institutions were turned down while four hundred thousand dollars, in initial funds were appropriated to construct the state capitol building with its gold-plated dome. Money did not come with the students, as tuition at first was "as free as the Colorado sunshine."

The senior class size at the University of Colorado dwindled from six in 1882, to two in 1883, to one in 1884. The dropout rate was blamed on the lure and availability of high-paying jobs. College-age men found work herding cattle or working in the mines for as much as one hundred dollars per month (more than three thousand dollars today)—almost as much as the monthly salary that Mary received as a full professor.

Of the three students who planned to graduate in 1885, one died; the second, a sister of the deceased, was so distraught that she was unable to continue her studies; and the third, according to a newspaper account, "did not quite succeed in finishing the prescribed course." A Master of Arts degree was conferred upon Ernest Pease, who had visited Mary in Paris, but he was not present. Two medical school students did receive their degrees.

A *Rocky Mountain News* article reflected on the melancholy commencement day of June 1885. One reporter wrote,

When President Sewall stepped onto the platform to announce the opening prayer, the small auditorium was but fairly filled, and on the platform was a long row of empty seats . . . The board of regents, which had been in session the day before, was conspicuous by its absence, and some of the members of the faculty might have been found about the building somewhere. As for the prominent citizens of the city and state, they were not there. On the whole there was a painful lack of interest in the commencement which made it a tame affair and rather flat as compared with other commencements.

Taxpayers questioned the employment of a full faculty when they did not see expected results. Mary still received her fourteen-hundred-dollar annual salary, but the men's salaries were lowered and fixed at eighteen hundred dollars. As president, Joseph Sewall took the blame, and the lack of operating capital drove him to despair. He later said that his life at that time was "filled with sadness, disappointment, and sorrow." The next year he turned in his resignation.

The following November, regent Horace Hale was appointed president but asked that Sewall remain as acting president until the graduation of Sewall's daughter Jennie in June 1887.

One day during the last few weeks of his presidency, Joseph Sewall met Mary in Old Main. She followed him up the long flight of stairs where he paused several times, seemingly lost in thought. Outside the window, young apple trees had begun to bloom, and spring rains had turned the grass from a dull brown to a soft light green.

At the time, Sewall's future was uncertain, but he wanted to make sure Mary's was secure, so he wrote her an open letter of recommendation. On May 3, 1887, he removed one of his last sheets of university letterhead from his desk drawer, dipped his pen into his inkwell, and wrote:

Miss Rippon has filled the chair of German and French Language and Literature nine years in this institution. She has proved herself to be thoroughly efficient as a teacher. Not only possessing an extended knowledge of the languages taught, but a remarkable power of imparting, and at the same time rousing an interest—an enthusiasm—in the student. The results of her labor here are more than satisfactory. The

Board of Regents—the whole faculty—as well as patrons and students unite in testimony to her ability, devotion, and above all, to her exalted womanhood. Should she sever her connection here it would be of her own choice.

The letter is remarkable because it demonstrates not only that Mary was an exemplary professor but that she had also lived up to Sewall's high moral standards. Sewall knew that Mary's classes continued to study the works of author Johann Wolfgang von Goethe, and his reference to "her exalted womanhood" coincided with Goethe's ideal of purity—expressed in his drama, *Faust*, as the "woman eternal." Sewall saw Mary as an accomplished professional in a man's world, but he also placed her on a pedestal as a woman.

* * *

Despite the financial and administrative turmoil at the university, classes went on as usual. A dedicated teacher, Mary made sure she took the time to become invested in her students. Timothy Stanton, who graduated in 1883, later stated, "She made it her pleasant duty to know every student individually, to learn his weaknesses and foibles that needed correction, and especially to learn his good qualities, too, that they might be cultivated and developed. This was all done so quietly and tactfully that she won the instant respect of every young man and woman in the school."

In addition to teacher–student relationships in the classroom, Mary also enjoyed social occasions with her students. She was a faithful member of the Phi Chapter of Delta Gamma, called a fraternity even though it was strictly a women's organization. The first time she attended, she and seven young ladies sat down for an elegant dinner at Ella Tyler Whiteley's house on Pine Street. Afterward, Mary was officially initiated as an honorary member while one of her students, with an obvious sense of humor, played Chopin's *Funeral March* on the piano. The young ladies held her in high esteem. The chapter secretary wrote to their national magazine, *Anchora*, "We have received many congratulations upon obtaining as a member one so eminent as Miss Ripon [*sic*], who is a lady of rare culture."

Figure 12.1. This photograph of Mary dates from the mid-1880s, around the time that she joined Delta Gamma.

Meanwhile, Sewall moved his family to Denver, where he had accepted the position of professor of chemistry at the University of Denver, and Horace Hale took over the presidency. More trees were planted, a pond was formed in the dammed-up ravine, and the cattle fence and stile were removed. No longer did Mary and her women students have to lift their long skirts to climb over the fence on their way to classes.

During the first decade of her tenure, Mary rose from a high school instructor to full professor and chair of the modern language department. She was the only female professor at the university and was acclaimed by her colleagues. Nationwide, female educators at the university and college level remained a rarity. Even with Sewall's glowing letter of recommendation, Mary must have been concerned about retaining her faculty position.

When Sewall left the university, Mary was thirty-seven. Besides advancing and excelling as a pioneer in her field, she held, and was determined to keep, the admiration and respect of her students—a goal that would be seriously threatened by an incoming student named Will Housel.

PART 3

HIDDEN YEARS, 1887–1893

Chapter 13

Will Housel, a handsome young man with brown hair and intense brown eyes, enrolled in Mary's German class in the fall of 1887. Several years earlier, Will had taken a few classes in the university's preparatory department, but he stayed only a short time. He then worked for a year or two and attended a school in the Midwest. When he returned to Boulder, he entered the university as a four-year bachelor's degree candidate in the Department of Philosophy and the Arts. The degree requirements at the time included four courses of Latin and Greek and two each of mathematics, rhetoric, oratory, and German.

Will came from a prominent Boulder family. His father, Peter Housel, had operated a grist mill, was an elder in the Boulder Valley Presbyterian Church, and served as Boulder County's first judge. According to Mary's student Ernest Pease, who had grown up in Will's neighborhood, the Housel family was "well-educated and had more books in their home than anyone else."

Like the others in Mary's class, Will's introduction to German was in grammar and pronunciation. Then he could begin the study of literature. Germany was still considered the educational and cultural center of the world, so a study of German literature was regarded as a necessary part of one's education. In the spring of 1888, after Will had signed up again, Mary led his German literature class through the usual study of Goethe's classic drama *Faust*. According to newspaper editor Amos Bixby, who still visited the campus and reported on the goings-on from time to time, German literature students longed for the time when "Mephistopheles no longer [was] a painted Devil but a sentient presence whom you are perfectly conscious is ready at any moment to drive a sharp bargain for your soul."

Translation practice included the *Song of the Spirits* in which Mephistopheles conjured up a vision to lull the character Faust to sleep. It began with the lines "Melt, ye confining vaults up yonder!" and led into Faust's revelation of nature, the cosmos, and spiritual beauty. The spirits hypnotized Faust by praising sensuality and relaxed his inhibitions by singing:

> Yield to the shining
> Ether's fonder
> Cerulean gaze!
> Cloudbanks darkling
> Dwindle for sparkling
> Starlets winking,
> Milder sun-rays
> Drinking the haze!
> Heavenly offspring's
> Graces uplifting,
> Swaying and turning,
> Drifting they wander,
> Lovelorn yearning
> Follows them yonder
> And their garments'
> Fluttering garlands
> Cover the far lands,
> Cover the arbor
> Where thought-rapt lover
> Lifelong trusting
> Pledges to lover
> Arbor to Arbor.

With Mary's dedication to teaching, it is likely that she gave Will individual attention. They probably discussed the themes in *Faust* as the story unfolded. Dr. Faust, Goethe's main character, determined to plumb the depths of how it felt to be human.

Figure 13.1. William C. "Will" Housel modestly wrote on his passport application that his features were "common." He enrolled in two of Mary's German classes.

At twenty-five, Will was a few years older than his classmates. He lived with his parents on their farm at Seventy-Fifth Street and Arapahoe Avenue, a few miles east of Boulder. Each day he rode his horse to the university, stabling him in the wagon shed behind Old Main.

By this time, Mary had purchased a sidesaddle and a horse named Fanny. Often Mary rode her horse and looked for wildflowers, just as she had done earlier with horses rented from the livery. Even when riding, Mary dressed like a lady in custom-made clothing. Society's restrictions in the Victorian era dictated a tight-fitting bodice over a corset with voluminous skirts and even a bustle extending the yards of material on the back of the skirt.

It is possible that Mary and Will rode together as she and Winthrop Scarritt had done. At any rate, their teacher–student relationship evolved into a friendship, and at some point, even with all the clothing, the friendship escalated into a romance.

No one will ever know the details of Mary and Will's relationship during this time. In the spring of 1888, Mary boarded at the home of

Figure 13.2. Will and Mary rode their horses on undeveloped prairie land now known as University Hill.
AUTHOR'S COLLECTION

a rancher who informed her that he and his wife would be gone from Boulder for a few weeks in order to drive their cattle down from higher pastures in North Park. Perhaps Mary and Will took that opportunity to become lovers.

Mary kept meticulous diaries year after year, yet none from this time period have survived. However, an undated poem, possibly the only written evidence of their intimacy, was stuck into a later diary. It read:

> We smiled and stood together for awhile,
> swift impulse made us do it.
> Your hand reached out toward mine,
> your kindly hand.
> Or was my hand the first?
> What did it matter?
> We knew and shared the solitude of crowds,
> Lofting above the clatter.

Like Faust, Mary had stepped outside the bounds of morality. Considering the prominence she had achieved in her profession and the idealized role model she had become, her actions were extraordinarily risky.

CHAPTER 14

IN THE EYES OF THE LORD, MARY WAS A SINNER, FOREVER MARRIED IN the flesh. She had returned to the Congregational Church, whose doctrine was clearly stated in a 1906 sermon: "No matter how it has been brought about, whether as the result of the highest spiritual affinity or of the basest brute passions, when this physical basis shall have been established, a new entity has been wrought, divinely recognized, humanly indissoluble. The twain are henceforth one flesh, whether they be of one spirit or not."

Mary may have imagined Joseph Sewall, on a nearly equal position with God, pointing at her and declaring, as he did on the university's opening day, "What we do is what we are." He had entrusted her with the morals of her female students and even praised her "exalted womanhood." Her actions belied her unblemished reputation.

If Mary had questions about sexual relations, she could have looked them up in medical texts in the library room in Old Main. One popular book, *Ladies' Guide to Health and Disease,* discussed women "whose lapses of virtue are known only to themselves and their companions in sin." According to the author, the only safeguard for virtue was religion, preferably Protestantism.

Mary's day-to-day routine remained unchanged. In addition to teaching, she went to Delta Gamma meetings and often visited with the Bracketts and the Bells. She particularly enjoyed the company of Delphine Bell, who arranged to leave her children for meetings of the Boulder Fortnightly Club.

In May 1888, Mary hosted an alumni dinner for faculty and former students in Old Main. The spring semester was almost over. On

May 25, Mary celebrated her thirty-eighth birthday. By this time, she probably was aware that she was pregnant. No doubt it was a time of soul-searching for her and for Will.

Considering the extensive correspondence Mary carried on throughout her life, she must have written to Auntie, in Illinois. Mary had been old enough to remember when Auntie's first son had been born, too soon after she and Uncle were married. Auntie would understand her predicament. Mary undoubtedly also wrote to Anna in Germany. From the choices Mary made as her pregnancy progressed, it was evident she knew she would leave Boulder to have the baby.

Victorian society had no place for an unmarried mother with a professional career. Mothers were expected to stay home, raise their children, and be supported by their husbands. According to the literature of the day, a man's prerequisites for marriage were a savings account and a career. Will had neither. He was still a student, and Mary was the one with an income.

Adding to the dilemma was the undisputed fact that Mary was a role model for her female students and highly acclaimed in her career. If her pregnancy were discovered, she must have believed that she would bring disgrace not only to herself but to all aspiring female educators.

Within the twenty years since Mary had graduated from Normal School, a few eastern colleges had opened exclusively for women. The female professors who taught them had formed a sisterhood of single women. M. Carey Thomas, Bryn Mawr's president, wrote of the plight of women who "spent half a lifetime in fitting themselves for their chosen work, then were asked to choose between it and marriage." According to the authors of *Women and Higher Education in American History*, the female professors' slogan was "Our failures only marry."

Mary's last social engagement of the school year was June 1. The members of the Boulder Fortnightly Club got together for a final meeting before formally disbanding for the season. Mary was surrounded by friends, almost all of them experienced mothers, but she could not ask questions about her condition or about what to expect during childbirth. It had to have been a lonely time.

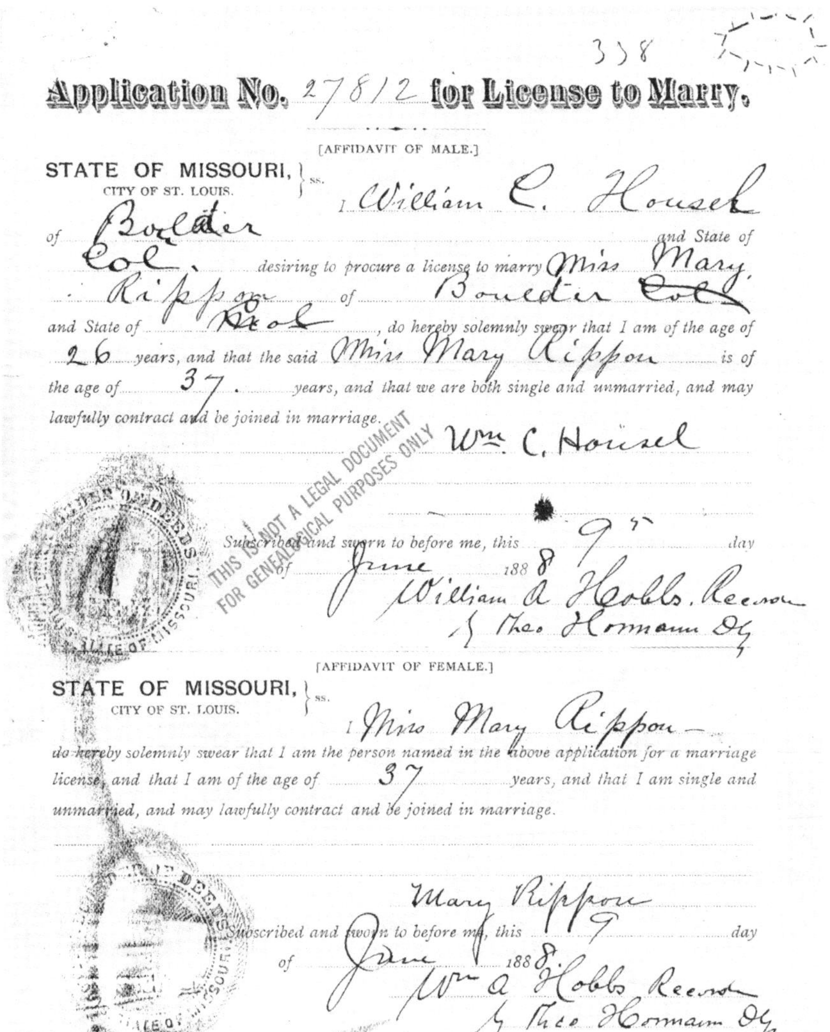

338

Application No. 27812 **for License to Marry.**

[AFFIDAVIT OF MALE.]

STATE OF MISSOURI, } ss.
CITY OF ST. LOUIS.

I William C. Housel of Boulder and State of Col. desiring to procure a license to marry Miss Mary Rippon of Boulder ~~Col~~ and State of Col, do hereby solemnly swear that I am of the age of 26 years, and that the said Miss Mary Rippon is of the age of 37. years, and that we are both single and unmarried, and may lawfully contract and be joined in marriage.

Wm. C. Housel

Subscribed and sworn to before me, this 9th day of June 1888

William A Hobbs, Recorder
by Theo Hormann Dy

[AFFIDAVIT OF FEMALE.]

STATE OF MISSOURI, } ss.
CITY OF ST. LOUIS.

I Miss Mary Rippon do hereby solemnly swear that I am the person named in the above application for a marriage license, and that I am of the age of 37 years, and that I am single and unmarried, and may lawfully contract and be joined in marriage.

Mary Rippon

Subscribed and sworn to before me, this 9 day of June 1888.

Wm A Hobbs Recorder
by Theo Hormann Dy

Figure 14.1. When giving their ages for their marriage license application, Mary took off a year and Will added a year.

ST. LOUIS CITY RECORDER OF DEEDS

Figure 14.2. Mary and Will's marriage license only required Will to be "over the age of twenty-one years" and Mary to be "over the age of eighteen years."

Although only five years had elapsed since Mary had taken a sabbatical, she asked the regents for another. She had experienced frequent bouts of neuralgia and respiratory problems, so she claimed that her need for a year off was to improve her health. The regents said they would take time to consider her request.

Ladies' Guide to Health and Disease stated, "For a woman to marry a man younger than herself is to prepare her for domestic unhappiness in the lack of the husband's power to command proper respect from his wife on account of his own inferiority in years and development." Even so, Mary and Will chose to legitimize their child.

As soon as the semester was over, Mary and Will took separate trains to St. Louis, Missouri. There, on June 9, 1888, in the Recorder of Deeds office, they signed a marriage application with affidavits stating they were "single and unmarried." Will gave his age as twenty-six, although he was still twenty-five, and Mary stated that she was thirty-seven, even though she had just turned thirty-eight.

That same day, they were united by clergy as Mr. and Mrs. William C. Housel. Their marriage license was duly recorded in the Office of Recorder of Deeds, St. Louis, Missouri, and filed in book 35, page 338. Other than the clergyman and the recorder, there were no witnesses.

CHAPTER 15

A TRAIN CARRIED THE NEWLYWEDS NORTHEAST INTO MARY'S NATIVE state of Illinois. Auntie and Uncle had moved from Fairbury to a farm just south of the neighboring town of Forest. The farm may have seemed a strange place for a wedding night, but it was far away from Boulder.

This period of Mary's life was unlike any other she had known. She and Will lived openly as husband and wife. Will found work on the farm while Auntie altered some of her own confinement clothing to fit Mary in the coming months.

As the days turned into weeks, Mary must have become anxious about her future. Finally, during the end of July, she received a notice in the mail that the regents had granted her a year's leave of absence "on account of ill health." As she loosened her corsets, Mary knew she did not have much time until Victorian society would expect her to remove her changing body from the eyes of strangers. Pregnant women were supposed to "withdraw to the supreme source of a woman's identity and purpose—the home." But Mary had no home.

Instead, with her future uncertain, she climbed aboard the next train to New York and eventually crossed the sea to Anna in Germany. Will had to return to Boulder to complete his degree.

Diary entries from other ocean crossings reveal that Mary usually was seasick on ocean voyages but probably never so much as on that crossing. When she was well enough, she went to the ladies' salon and wrote letters. Included in her regular correspondence were Will, Auntie and Uncle, Joseph Sewall, Delphine Bell, and the Delta Gamma girls. Periodically she wrote to the *Boulder County Herald* and the university newspaper so they could print news of her travels. It was evident that she thought it important to keep her students and colleagues informed of her whereabouts, even though she did not reveal the real reason for her journey.

No letters or diaries survive from this very personal time in Mary's life, but it is safe to assume that she poured out her heart to Anna as soon as she reached Hannover. Anna probably was next to Mary during the quickening. As Mary felt the baby move inside of her for the first time, she must have been gripped with her new responsibility. Physically she may have felt better than in her early stage of pregnancy, but it was likely that she could not escape the constant crashing of the waves that went on in her mind. What would she do with the baby?

For a short time, Mary could wear her same dresses, with a loosened corset, and still go to concerts and museums. Then, as her body changed, she remained in Anna's home, reading, sewing, and writing letters. When she received a letter from Auntie, Mary learned that Uncle had died of typhoid fever, the same illness that had claimed her father. A handsome monument was placed on his grave in the flat prairie cemetery just outside of Fairbury. Mary had lost her favorite uncle, the man who helped to raise her and who had fought in court for her inheritance. She could not even join with Auntie and other family members to mourn their loss.

At some point in her confinement, Mary did venture out of Anna's house to travel by train to Stuttgart. Why she chose to go there remains a mystery. Anna probably went with her. When they arrived, there was little to do but wait and write more letters. Mary sent one of her newsy notes to the *Boulder County Herald* that, on January 9, 1889, reported, "Miss Rippon is now at Stuttgart, Germany."

Mary probably remembered little about her baby's birth. If she had a modern doctor-assisted delivery, the doctor would have held a cloth with chloroform over her nose and mouth as her labor pains intensified.

When she woke up, Will's brown eyes stared at her from the bundled-up baby girl at her side. Mary named her daughter Miriam Edna Housel. Most likely, Miriam was for her childhood friend, Miriam Barstow Massey. Mary had achieved what the ladies' magazines called "the fulfillment of a woman's physiological and moral destiny." The date was January 17, 1889.

Figure 15.1. Miriam Edna Housel was born in Stuttgart, Germany, on January 17, 1889. This unidentified photograph, believed to be of Miriam, was donated with Mary's diaries to the university.

Mary, Miriam, and, most likely, Anna, stayed in Stuttgart until Mary felt well enough to travel. Mary wrote to the editor of the *University Portfolio*, who reported in the next issue of the student newspaper, "On account of ill health, our Professor in French and German, Miss Rippon, is spending the year abroad. May her speedy recovery cause her to return to us at an early day, in safety and happiness."

Meanwhile, Mary exchanged letters with Delphine Bell. Delphine had written of her family's move from Boulder to Geneva, Switzerland, where her husband, James, was engaged in literary work. Three months after Miriam's birth, Mary paid them a visit, documented by her dated signature in Delphine's ten-year-old daughter's autograph book.

Obviously, Mary considered Delphine a very close friend. Bell descendants have related that Delphine passed on the circumstances of Miriam's birth, so it is likely that Delphine and her family were acquainted with the baby at this time. Delphine soon would deliver her fifth (fourth living) child. Finally, Mary had a trusted friend, another mother, with whom she could talk about feedings, illnesses, sleeping habits, and all the details of infant care.

No one knows how Mary took to motherhood or what kinds of feelings she had for her daughter at this time. If she bonded with Miriam, it is hard to imagine how she could ever have considered leaving her. Mary may, instead, have kept an emotional distance. Her emotions probably went into letters, long since lost or destroyed, to Anna or to Will.

Chapter 16

As the spring semester of 1889 neared an end, Will prepared for his graduation. Soft breezes blew through Old Main with the fragrance of wild plums and apple trees. Wildflowers had burst into bloom all over the prairies and partway up the canyons.

Will and his only classmate, Delta Gamma member Helen Beardsley, decided to leave their mark on the university by planting ivy on the northeast side of Old Main. In honor of Class Day, the day before Commencement, Will wrote a poem. It expressed his love of trees and flowers and read:

> But seems there is a legend, or an old philosophy,
> That a spirit sometimes lingers in a blossom or a tree.
> If it is not so, how is it that the human heart can see
> Something there that wakes an answer
> like a thrill of sympathy?
> Weeping willow, modest violet and the pansy think-of-me,
> Laurel signalizes glory, and the broom humility.
> But the ivy is for friendship, and it seemeth best of all,
> 'Tis the rose of love with petals that will never fade or fall.
> And as friendship, saith the poet,
> is but "love without his wings,"
> Ivy is its chosen symbol for it closest, longest clings—
> Clings when others have departed;
> clings about the ruined heap;
> When forgotten human friends are
> wrapped in their eternal sleep.

So let others plant their elm trees to betray their dignity,
Or a sturdy oak to blazon unsuspected bravery;
But the Senior class is going to plant an ivy vine
In the empty northeast corner,
where the morning sun may shine.
There, where the college building
breaks the western zephyr's will,
That sometimes blows the boulders
towards the ruins of the mill.
Long may the college flourish, long flourish the ivy too;
For the one will robe the other in a beauty yearly new.
And as coming generations through the institution pass,
May the greenness of the ivy contrast with the Senior Class.
And may bonds of endless friendship symboled by the ivy vine,
Grow between the Alma Mater and the class of '89.

Will may have enclosed a copy of his poem in one of his letters to Mary. Their love of flowers was something they had in common. Within a few weeks, Will would join his wife and child in Switzerland. One- and two-line news items on the comings and goings of Boulder residents were published every week in the local newspapers. The *Boulder County Herald Weekly* announced that Will had received his passport and planned to leave for Europe right after graduation.

Boulder residents were further informed when Will arrived in Geneva in June. By then, Miriam was five months old. Again, the family's reunion can only be imagined. How did Will like Miriam? Was it awkward for Mary and Will, after ten months apart, to live again as a married couple? These questions will always remain unanswered.

After a period of adjustment, Mary and Will must have spent a considerable amount of time discussing their future. Only two months remained in Mary's sabbatical leave. She and Will had little time to decide what to do with Miriam.

On Will's passport application, he had listed his occupation as "student" and wrote that he intended to return to the United States "within five years." This statement indicates that in their correspondence in preceding months, he and Mary must have discussed the possibility of his remaining overseas for some time and attending a European graduate school. But what of little Miriam?

Will had no job and little money. Finally, Mary and Will decided to place Miriam in a nearby Catholic orphanage. Mary's diary provides no additional details, but the religious institution accepted children whose parents were unable to care for them as well as children whose parents were deceased. With Miriam under the care of the Sisters and Will in the same city, Mary could return to Colorado to teach.

By carefully managing her salary, Mary could afford to send money for both Will's tuition and for Miriam's care. The idea of a Victorian wife financially supporting her husband and family was highly unusual, but Mary's private life was anything but conventional.

Whether the arrangement was meant to be temporary or permanent is unknown, but Mary wrote to her students in Boulder and informed them she would be home for the beginning of the school year. She probably visited Anna in Hannover before sailing on the SS *Belgenland* that left Antwerp, Belgium, on August 3, 1889.

The Delta Gammas were excited about Mary's impending return. Their secretary wrote in their national publication, *Anchora*, "With pleasure we learn that Miss Mary Rippon will be with us again next year. Our institution has been long enough without a mother, and orphandom has been sorely felt in many ways . . . Pretty souvenirs postmarked 'Geneva' only prove once more the interest Miss Rippon ever takes in her students. Bright or dull, rich or poor, it matters not. All receive like attention. Do you wonder that we deplore her vacancy in the faculty and long for her return?"

Obviously, the Delta Gammas considered Mary a very caring woman. It is ironic that they deplored being "without a mother" while thirty-nine-year-old Mary left her own baby and husband on a dock in a foreign land.

On board the ship, Mary was one of thirty-six first-class passengers, mostly Americans. They ate and slept separately from the Europeans who made up the second class. Nearly three hundred immigrants were below, in the steerage, where accommodations were least expensive.

Figure 16.1. In August 1889, Mary left Will and Miriam in Germany and sailed to New York on the SS *Belgenland* of the Red Star American Line.
PEABODY ESSEX MUSEUM, SALEM, MASSACHUSETTS

Thirteen days after leaving Antwerp, the SS *Belgenland* docked in New York. Excited passengers cheered when they first viewed the colossal 152-foot statue titled "Liberty Enlightening the World." The recently unveiled statue was a gift from France and intended to commemorate the French and American revolutions. To Mary and other returning Americans, Liberty meant the end of their long journeys home. Immigrants saw the statue as a symbol of new opportunities in a new land. Liberty, who was strikingly similar to Goethe's woman eternal, held a tablet in her left arm, while in her uplifted right hand she grasped a torch as if lighting the world.

The bustle and activity in New York City was a sharp contrast to the open sea. Freight wagons, hacks, and carriages moved night and day through the narrow streets crisscrossed by hundreds of electric and telegraph lines which tied together the endless crowded buildings.

Figure 16.2. The printing firm of Currier & Ives depicted "The great Bartholdi statue, Liberty Enlightening the World" in this hand-colored lithograph, circa 1885.

According to passenger lists, Mary was the first to debark. When asked to give her age, she subtracted four years as she had on her last trip with Helen Coleman. Continuing this little lie may have made her more confident of handling her much bigger secret.

On the way west, Mary got off the train in Fairbury and spent a few days with Auntie. Together they visited Uncle's grave, which is still marked with an impressive *S* for Skinner, intertwined with his initials *W. W.* Then Mary was back on the train to Boulder.

The *Boulder County Herald* announced Mary's arrival by stating, "Mary Rippon, Professor of German and French, has been connected with the University eleven years. Professor Rippon is returning from her second extended trip to Germany and France and will give to the students the benefit of her mature and cultivated mind."

Biologically she was a mother to Miriam, but at the university she was expected to be "mother" to her students. Could she be both at the same time?

Chapter 17

Mary was warmly received by her students after her year abroad. She concentrated on their studies, but her mind may have wandered. After translations in one of her French literature classes, a student wrote in the school newspaper, "It seems to be the genuine verdict of the whole class (teacher and all) that 'love stories' are preferable any day to 'dry' history." Will was not forgotten.

The ivy that Will and his classmate had recently planted grew just outside Mary's classroom window. She may have imagined his presence from his poem that proclaimed, "A spirit sometimes lingers in a blossom or a tree." The trees had grown enough that their leaves shaded and softened the lines of Old Main.

Mary was not the only professor at the university to have returned from Europe in the fall of 1889. Dr. James Bell had finished his work in Switzerland and moved back to Boulder with his wife Delphine and their family. New daughter Geneva had been named for the city of her birth and was four months old. If Mary and Will had planned to keep their marriage and child a secret from everyone in Boulder, they could do so no longer. The Bells already knew the truth.

The two old friends lost no time getting involved in their former club and church activities. Mary and Delphine were honored at an afternoon tea given by the Boulder Fortnightly Club members. Shortly afterward, they all met in their new "Club Room" over the First National Bank on Pearl Street.

Everyone brought their own chairs, and they filled the shelves with books borrowed from the University library. The Delta Gamma's meeting room was next door. Mary spent many afternoons with the young ladies who jokingly called her "Mother." Mary, perhaps accompanied by the Bell family, continued to attend services of the Congregational church.

While Mary continued to teach in Boulder, Will began a philosophy course at the University of Leipzig in Germany. Presumably, Miriam was in an orphanage in the same city. No one will ever know how Mary felt about being separated from her child, but she must have been torn between her family and her career. At least she could talk with Delphine, and she could write her feelings to Anna, Auntie, and Will.

As in the past, Mary again taught Goethe's *Faust*. Some of the passages may have taken on a new meaning for her, especially the "Doctrine of Two Souls:"

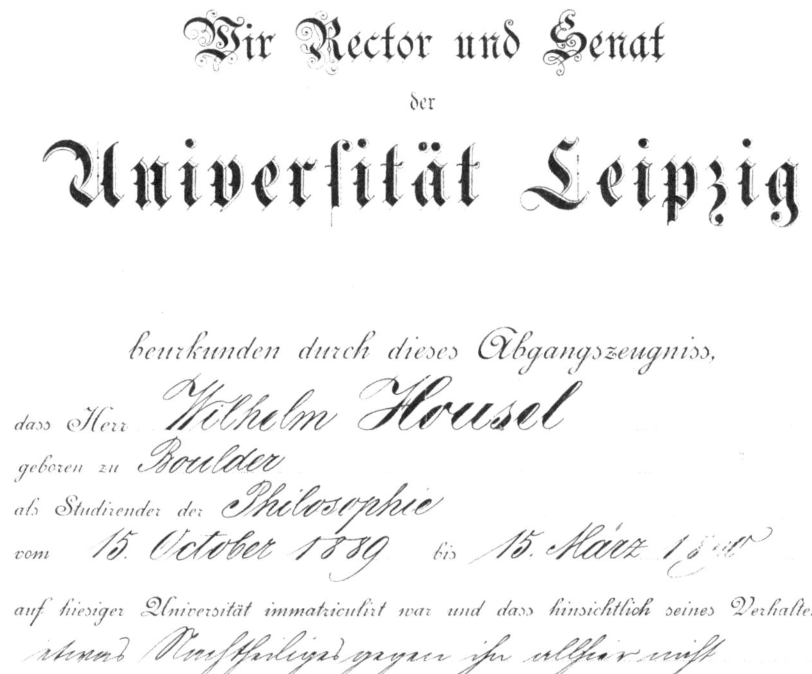
Wir Rector und Senat
der
Universität Leipzig

beurkunden durch dieses Abgangszeugniss,
dass Herr Wilhelm Housel
geboren zu Boulder
als Studirender der Philosophie
vom 15. October 1889 bis 15. März 18
auf hiesiger Universität immatriculirt war und dass hinsichtlich seines Verhaltens
etwas Nachtheiliges gegen ihn allhier nicht

Figure 17.1. "Wilhelm Housel" of Boulder, studied philosophy at the University of Leipzig from October 15, 1889 to March 15, 1890.
AUTHOR'S COLLECTION

Two souls, alas, are dwelling in my breast,
And either would be severed from its brother;
The one holds fast with joyous earthly lust
Onto the world of man with organs clinging;
The other soars impassioned from the dust,
To realms of lofty forebears winging.

Mary was as close to Will as the telegraph office. The two planned for emergencies and even created their own secret code so that no one in the Boulder telegraph office would understand an incoming or outgoing message. Mary preserved the code on a single sheet of paper, probably torn from a since-destroyed diary.

Neatly handwritten were the following words and their explanations:

Ivory—Come at once.

Jasper—Miriam is ill.

Despot—$100 by telegram.

Facile—$100 by letter.

Sent—On the way.

Broker—Will start as soon as possible.

These words were followed by Will's pseudonym, "Harvest," suitable for a farm boy but uncommon for a student of language and philosophy.

Will was in Germany when his mother, Eliza Steuart Housel, died of pneumonia on Christmas morning, 1889. Her obituary in the *Boulder News* announced her funeral at Columbia (also called Pioneer) Cemetery. Many times, Mary had ridden by the small treeless cluster of gravestones on her way to the canyons west of the university. Eliza Housel may have known Mary as her son's professor, but it is unlikely that she knew of Mary and Will's marriage or of her own little granddaughter overseas. The Boulder newspapers reported the funeral as one of the largest in the county.

Then, suddenly, Delphine's thirty-four-year-old husband, Dr. James Bell, also contracted pneumonia. Because of his previous lung ailment, his condition immediately turned serious. Dr. Bell, then chair of the Department of Greek and Psychology, died just two weeks after Will's mother. He, too, was buried in Columbia Cemetery.

Left behind with thirty-six-year-old Delphine were eleven-year-old Rosetta, nine-year-old William, five-year-old Cleophile, eight-month-old Geneva, and an unborn child.

Miriam's first birthday fell during the week after James Bell's death. In Mary's diary, on January 17, 1890, she simply wrote, "M.'s day."

* * *

Mary continued to teach. Although her position did not change, each year brought visible changes to the evolving campus. A new men's dormitory, Woodbury Hall, was under construction on the east side of Old Main. In the spring, buds on the purple lilacs swelled and burst into bloom. Their gentle fragrance and color blended with the pink and white blossoms of the apple and plum trees along the edge of University Pond. A railroad on the east side of the campus brought trains from Denver to the university's own depot.

Meanwhile, two of Mary's female students had arranged a year of study overseas and needed a shipboard traveling companion. Mary agreed to go and promised her other students she would return at the end of the summer. No one in Boulder, except Delphine, knew she would spend the intervening time with Will and Miriam.

Mary and the two young ladies boarded a Union Pacific Denver & Gulf train at Boulder's new stone depot on Fourteenth Street. Instead of heading north for Cheyenne, they took the southbound train to Denver—the largest railroad station in the West. Mary and the young ladies transferred to a Pullman sleeping car that took them through Kansas on their way to the East. At night, a porter transformed each of their seats into beds. They were rocked to sleep by the constant motion of the train.

If the young ladies questioned Mary about the ocean, she may have compared it to the waves in the tall grass on the seemingly endless prairie. Gradually the high plains gave way to cultivated fields, and then to farms separated by hedgerows. Small railroad stops were replaced by larger towns. Mary and her charges changed trains again in Chicago on their way to New York City.

No personal details survive from Mary's journey in the summer of 1890. Because of her responsibility to her students, she would have safely escorted them to their destination before setting out on her own. Will, as handsome as ever, probably met her at the train station in Germany. With him would have been Miriam, a toddler who would have thought her a stranger. This time it was Mary's turn to get reacquainted. But what of her marriage to Will?

Wherever they went, whether in museums or in the mountains, Will and Mary had to have discussed their future plans. Before the summer's end, it is obvious that they decided to keep the arrangement they had made the previous year. Mary would return to Boulder to teach and earn a salary. Will would stay near Miriam and attend graduate school, this time at the University of Geneva. According to his *Livret d'Etudiant,* or student book, he signed up for political systems, sociology, comparative literature, and two philosophy classes. He wrote his former Boulder classmates that he had become quite a linguist and improved his knowledge of Spanish, Italian, Swedish, German, and French.

A loose page from one of Mary's diaries shows that when she returned to Boulder, she sent both dollars and francs overseas. It appears to have been for Miriam's care as well as for Will's tuition. Mary also had other family responsibilities. In November, she returned to her childhood home of Lisbon Center, Illinois, and oversaw the burial of her late grandfather's widow who had recently died of cancer. Mary purchased a plot near her father and grandfather in the Lisbon Cemetery. She hired furniture dealer and undertaker Stillman Massey, husband of her childhood friend Miriam, to prepare the body for interment.

Mary's schedule, in the fall of 1890, became too much for her to handle. In an effort to increase enrollment, President Hale had advertised for and attracted new students. Mary's course load included ten German classes as well as several in French. The first to go was her beginning French class. The university newspaper reported that the cancellation disappointed her students.

Meanwhile, unannounced visitors still sat in her German classes to observe her teaching. In February 1891, state legislator L. B. Schwanbeck reported to the press:

> I was surprised; indeed I was delighted, with the work done. For a class of American pupils to take up Goethe's *Faust* where they did and translate it as fluently and as correctly as was done, surpassed my expectation. It showed not only that the lady [Miss Rippon] was well-versed in German herself, but that she has her pupils well in hand and knows how to get study out of them. The University should have as liberal support as the state can possibly afford, and it should be fostered without a stint.

Obviously, Mary was pleased at this recognition as she preserved the newspaper clipping with her diaries, where it remained untouched for more than a century.

Before the end of the school year, Mary knew that she would have to make additional cuts in her schedule. She asked the regents if Delphine could assist her by teaching the remainder of her French classes.

The unspoken rule against a married woman, especially one with a child or children, working as a professional only applied to those who had a husband. Delphine was now a widow and the sole supporter of her five children. In addition, Delphine had grown up in a midwestern colony of French Canadians, so French was her native language. According to the *University Portfolio*, the regents accepted her on the faculty as "an experienced teacher and a lady of high attainments and culture." They added, "Her connection with the institution cannot but add very materially to the efficiency of its excellent corps of instructors."

More advances for women were made that academic year. Miss Caroline Hyde had recently been hired as an instructor of Latin. Mary was still the only professor, but with the addition of the lady instructors, Delphine Bell and Caroline Hyde, Mary was no longer the only woman on the faculty. Her title was changed from professor of German and French to professor of German language and literature.

Figure 17.2. Will sailed to New York after completing his studies at the University of Geneva. Miriam stayed in Switzerland alone.

The following summer, in 1891, Mary kept her travel plans to herself. A brief mention in the university newspaper of her return at the end of the summer is the only indication that she had ever left Boulder. But, she had.

When Miriam started to talk, she was taught to call her mother "Aunt Mary," and she continued to do so for the rest of her life. The circumstances surrounding Miriam's birth were, at the time, kept even from her.

Miriam's and Will's expenses, and Mary's yearly travels, severely stretched her still-meager income. She soon fell back on what she had learned as a child and began to loan money, with interest, to others. Mary started an account book and noted the funds she lent, and the interest due, to friends and former students.

During the summer of 1891, Mary and Will must have realized that their current arrangement could not go on indefinitely. Mary agreed to continue to support Miriam, but she no longer paid for Will's graduate school.

Meanwhile, Will's widowed father, Peter Housel, had recently married Louisa Wolcott, a widow with three sons. Louisa was described by a family member as "beautiful to look at and a devout Christian woman." It is likely that Peter had written to Will explaining that he needed help on the family farm. Will's mother's probate had been settled, and Will's inheritance was first choice of her horses.

Will left Miriam alone in Geneva and returned to Boulder—and to Mary.

CHAPTER 18

WILL'S FRIENDS WERE GLAD TO SEE HIM WHEN HE ARRIVED BACK IN Boulder in December 1891. The *Boulder County Herald* announced, "W. C. Housel, an old University boy, returned from the east last week. It is three years since he left Boulder, and during that time he has spent over two years in Europe, part of the time at Leipzig at school, part of the time taking in the sights as he traveled from place to place on a safety [bicycle]. He saw lots, had a good time, and has come to Boulder to locate."

Mary had moved into the stately three-story home of Colonel John and Lizzie Ellet located on four city lots southeast of the intersection of Walnut and Fourteenth streets. The house was private as it was surrounded by nearly one hundred young ornamental trees. For a few weeks while the Ellets visited their family in Saint Paul, Minnesota, Mary was in the big house alone.

Her marriage with Will, at this time, was like an affair. He lived with his father and step-mother on the Arapahoe Road farm. During the first six months of 1892, both Mary and Will kept separate diaries. The entries are brief and contain very little of their feelings, but their whereabouts can be easily correlated.

Will visited twice a week, usually on Sundays and Wednesdays. By then he was still a youthful twenty-nine-year old, but Mary was a graying forty-one. "Miss Rippon," as she was still called, had become so respected as a professor, and so revered as a role model, that it was out of the question that anyone would perceive an impropriety.

Still, Mary walked on dangerous ground. If Miriam's birth, or the current intimacies, had become known to the public, the resulting scandal would have rocked the community and caused Mary to resign in disgrace.

The feigning of virtues she no longer possessed may have been deeply troubling to Mary, but it is revealing that instead of ending the relationship, she continued it. Mary and Will managed to hide their marriage so well that Will's visits blended in with those of other former and current students.

Mary continued to teach and give her students individual attention. She met with President Hale, Delphine, and other faculty members. She still "mothered" the Delta Gammas and occasionally stayed overnight with the other young ladies in the women's cottage. She also managed to find time to attend church and prepare lectures for the Boulder Fortnightly Club.

Fellow friend and colleague Professor J. Raymond Brackett assisted Mary in her lectures by operating a lantern slide projector. In a history of the Fortnightly Club that Mary wrote many years later, she credited him with the difficult task of combining the exact amount of oxygen and ether to provide the projector's light source. She wrote, "The gases flickered and sometimes even exploded, but Mr. Brackett operated it so well that the audience was unaware of our problems."

According to the *Boulder County Herald Weekly*, Will was in the audience for Mary's talk on "Venice, City of the Sea." Just as the audience was unaware of her projector problems, they were unaware that Mary had a husband in the same room. When seen together in public, the couple probably avoided any suspicion of familiarity by falling back on their prior professor-student relationship.

Mary and Will led very different lives. Mary's daily activities centered on the university. While she was caught up in academic life, Will, according to his diary, spent his days hauling manure, slaughtering pigs, and mending fences. Although most of the time he worked on his father's farm, he spent a day or two at the Farmers' Institute in the nearby town of Longmont where Joseph Sewall appeared as a guest lecturer and spoke on "The Relation of Science to the Art of Farming."

After the Ellets returned, Will still visited Mary on Sundays and at least once during the week. Along with his pick of his mother's horses, he boarded Mary's horse Fanny at the Housel farm. The care of her horse may have given Mary and Will another legitimate reason to be seen together.

Little Miriam was not entirely forgotten. Her third birthday was on January 17, 1892. In her diary, Mary noted, "Miriam's birthday. Will came to dinner." Perhaps because Will lived with his father and step-mother, his diary entry was more guarded. For the same day he simply wrote "M.," the notation he wrote every time he visited Mary.

Sometime that winter or spring, Miriam was moved to an orphanage in Nice, France. A brief entry in Mary's diary, on May 16, 1892, was "Letter from France. M. [Miriam] better." At home, Colonel Ellet suffered a lingering illness. While Miriam was sick overseas, Mary's landlord died. He had been Boulder's former mayor, a temperance leader, and a pillar of the community.

Newspaper accounts detailed Ellet's funeral and stated that "sorrow hung like a pall over the city." The United States flag, with streamers of mourning, hung limp against the clock tower on the nearby red-brick courthouse. While the Colonel lay in his casket under a profusion of flowers, crowds of people gathered in the parlors of the Ellet home to pay their last respects. More than sixty carriages and buggies were backed up in all directions.

The day after the funeral Mary wrote in her diary, "Dr. Brackett came to take me home with him. Stayed all night. Will came to see me there." Within the next few days, Mary moved into the Bracketts' home. At some point—and the night of Colonel Ellet's funeral may have been the time—Mary and Will took the Bracketts into their confidence. From then on, the Bracketts joined Delphine Bell as trusted friends who knew and protected their secret.

Will still visited Mary, at least, on Sundays. The Congregational Church was down the street and around the corner from the Brackett home. According to their diaries, Mary and Will often were in attendance, although they probably did not sit together. With the friends who knew of her marriage, Mary seemed to have been much more at ease. One time Mary noted in her diary, "W. [Will] came. Went to see the Bells. Perfect day."

With their little daughter on the other side of the ocean and their marriage hidden from public view, however, Mary and Will faced an uncertain future.

One night in February 1892, Mary noted in her diary, "Went to Denver." Will's entry in his diary was, "Went to Denver. Warm." The next day, Mary did not make any entry in her diary, but Will wrote in his diary, "Came home this PM. Not much headway with the hard knot."

Without any more details, it is difficult to extrapolate the meaning of the "hard knot," but it is likely that Mary and Will spent the night together in a hotel in Denver where they discussed their marriage. Will may have tried to convince Mary to leave her position at the university. He may not have understood why teaching was so important to her when she had, and hid, a husband and child.

Chapter 19

As modest and unassuming as Mary was reported to have been, she must have been surprised to learn that her reputation and fame as a pioneer woman educator had spread to another institution. Three weeks after Will's notation in his diary of the "hard knot," Mary received a letter from a secretary at the University of Illinois, in Champaign. It was the university she had hoped to attend after high school, but at the time it had not accepted women. Suddenly, almost a quarter of a century later, the school offered her a teaching position *because* she was a woman.

The letter, dated March 9, 1892, read:

Dear Madam,

Would you, if it be found upon investigation that you are the woman to fill a chair in the University of Illinois, think of accepting? Of course, if you would not think of accepting, should you have an opportunity, it is not worthwhile for you to write me from what institution you have graduated, what positions you have held, etc., but if you do consider the matter favorably, write me definitely on these subjects.

Please let me hear from you immediately. Yours truly,

K. L. Kennard

The letter must have boosted Mary's self-esteem, as she preserved the job offer with other acknowledgments of her teaching career. She lost no time in writing her reply that revealed how happy she was with her career at the University of Colorado. It was obvious that she was in control of her professional and personal lives and did not need to flee a scandal nor to start over in another state.

On March 14 she responded:

> Your letter of March 9 was duly received. Your question is direct, and I shall endeavor to make my reply equally so. It is not worthwhile to consider me as a candidate for a chair in the University of Illinois. I have held my present position since the year in which the University of Colorado was opened and am too closely interested in the growth of the institution to wish to make a change. I am fitted for teaching only German and French. My work here is very pleasant and the Board of Regents very considerate in granting me from time to time leave of absence for travel and study.
>
> I feel a great interest in the University of my native state—Illinois—and wish you the best of success in your research for a woman to fill a chair. Thanking you for your letter. I remain.
>
> Very cordially yours, Mary Rippon

On the day of Mary's reply, she noted in her diary, "Replied to K. L. Kennard, Champaign, Ill." Will's only notation was, "Hauled hay to town." He appeared to have settled into the routine of life on the family farm. His father, Peter Housel, was sixty-eight years old and must have welcomed Will's assistance. In May, Will decided to buy the farm from his father, and he borrowed two hundred dollars from Mary for the down payment.

A month later, Mary gave Will an even more substantial loan. This was for the *Colorado Farmer and Livestock Journal*, a four-page agricultural newspaper based in Denver and devoted exclusively to farming and ranching all over the state. Even though Mary was the parent who continued to send money overseas for Miriam's care, she loaned Will nearly half of her annual salary. Mary's June 19, 1892, diary entry was, "Gave Will $600 to pay on *Colorado Farmer*."

The newspaper was the official organ of the state grange, horticultural society, and associations of poultry raisers, wool growers, and beekeepers. In addition to articles on poultry, farming, and other topics of interest to the associations' members, it included display advertisements for farm implements and classified advertisements for jobs, properties, and notices of stray livestock. Will's purchase of the *Journal* even was mentioned in the *Boulder County Herald Weekly*.

Will no longer had time to continue his diary. His entries stopped abruptly, but his activities can be traced through the entries in Mary's diary. Will continued to come to Boulder to visit her on Sundays. Sometimes they attended church. Mary noted that they wrote letters to each other during the week.

Since Mary rarely confided her thoughts or feelings in her diary, the brief comments, when they are found, are quite revealing. On August 19, 1892, Mary wrote, "Will came. Long sad talk." A few weeks later, she noted, "Will came. Hard day."

More than a year had passed since Mary had seen Miriam. The passage of time had been nearly that long for Will. Throughout the fall and winter of the 1892–1893 school year, Mary and Will maintained the uneasy equilibrium of their marital relationship. In October, Will paid back some of the money he had borrowed, then promptly borrowed some more. If the strain of Mary's separate lives had begun to take its toll, she hid it from her social contacts, worked effectively with her colleagues, and still gave individual instruction in the classroom. She continued to teach Faust and the other German language and literature classes and, above all, remained a role model for her female students.

In January 1893, Mary noted in her account book a twenty-dollar child support payment to Nice, France. Then, a month later, she made a related expenditure of three hundred dollars. When placed in the context of events to follow, this appears to have been for one round-trip and one one-way steamship ticket from Europe to the United States. Someone, probably Will, brought Miriam to America. After the February date in the account book, "Nice [France]" was written in once but crossed out with no explanation. Miriam had turned four years old.

Years later, after Miriam had grown up and applied for a passport in her own name, she wrote that she did not remember on which ship she sailed but thought she first came to America at the age of three. Whether she left a European port before or after her January 17 birthday is irrelevant. No longer would the ocean separate Miriam from Mary and Will.

CHAPTER 20

THE FIRST PLACE MIRIAM STAYED IN AMERICA PROBABLY WAS THE Saint Clara's Catholic Home for Girls in Denver. In Mary's account book, she made a notation for a charitable donation to a Denver "girls' home" in 1893, but no records from the home have survived.

Mary still paid for Miriam's care, but according to her diaries, she rarely visited her child. By this time, Will lived in Denver, so he could have more frequently visited Miriam, just as he was presumed to have done while attending graduate schools in Leipzig and Geneva. The child had to adjust to a new bed, new friends, new teachers, a new language, and a new country. She had never known a real home.

During the spring of 1893, Mary and Will's relationship became strained. After one of Will's less frequent visits to Boulder, Mary noted in her diary, "W. came. I was cross." In an undated notation, she added:

Opinions! Principles! And both are good!
Can two so disagree—and each be right?
I wonder! Can the white you see be black?
And can my black be white?

Despite the proximity to Miriam and the conflicts with Will, Mary taught a full schedule of classes. Overall attendance at the university had risen seventy-five percent over the previous year. Mary also spent many hours preparing a lecture on modern sculpture for an upcoming Boulder Fortnightly Club meeting. New lantern slides she incorporated into the program were described by a reporter as "a delightfully graphic style of description."

One day, after class, fellow professor and friend J. Raymond Brackett hauled his heavy camera and tripod up the long flight of stairs to Mary's classroom, then on the third floor of Old Main. He explained that a collection of photographs of the university would be exhibited in the Colorado Building at the upcoming Chicago World's Fair. He asked Mary to pose for him at her desk.

Before Mr. Brackett took the photograph, Mary wrote on the blackboard behind her:

Schwindet, ihr Dunkeln
Wolbungen Droben!

The words, in German, are the opening lines of Faust's "Song of the Spirits," in which the Devil, Mephistopheles, conjured up visions to relax Faust's inhibitions.

Mary's classes were over in June. On June 18, she wrote in her diary, "Morning with W. Very tired." The next day she "left early for Denver" and "took UP [Union Pacific Railroad] for Chicago" where she arrived on June 21. The following day, she went to the World's Fair.

Officially, the fair had been named the World's Columbian Exposition as it was built to celebrate the four-hundredth anniversary of Christopher Columbus's discovery of America. The exposition should have been held in 1892, but construction problems and wet weather delayed the opening for one year.

Fairgoers agreed that the "Dream City" was worth the wait. The *Portfolio of Photographic Views* stated that "Every lecturer and leader might feel sure of an hour of glory here." Mary probably enjoyed the Women's Building with its nationwide displays on Fortnightly Clubs. Elaborate walkways, stately buildings, and electrically illuminated fountains created a surreal fairyland.

During the preceding weeks, Miriam had been passed around an extended group of family and friends just as Mary had been as a child. Miriam may have started off with a visit on the farm with Auntie. At one point or another, someone had taken Miriam to Illinois, for on July 3, Miriam and Mary were reunited in Chicago at the fair. Mary wrote

Figure 20.1. Professor J. Raymond Brackett took this photograph of Mary in her classroom to display it with others at the Chicago World's Fair.

in her diary, "To the fair, met Miriam." The child had arrived with Jane Barstow, the mother of Mary's childhood friend Miriam Barstow Massey.

On July 6, Mary wrote, "Miriam and I went alone to Fair. Saw state buildings and art gallery." Perhaps the mother and her four-year-old daughter went to see the photographs of the university with Mary in her classroom. They may have ridden the gigantic Ferris wheel that took twenty minutes to revolve and held sixty passengers in each of its thirty-six coaches.

The next day, Miriam must have been left with Mrs. Barstow, as Mary took the train to Detroit to see her dressmaker and to visit with her aging tour leader, Mrs. L. H. Stone. When Mary returned to Chicago, she noted that she "Went to see M."

Mary still listed the dates of the letters she wrote and received from Will. Although none of these letters survive, property records relate the turn of events in Will's life. His father returned the two-hundred-dollar deposit Will had paid into the family farm, but instead of repaying his debt to Mary, Will invested it in four city lots in Boulder.

A few weeks later, Will sold his newly purchased lots. Around that time, he also sold the *Colorado Farmer and Livestock Journal*. It is not known if he offered Mary the return of her money, but he used it, or its equivalent, to resume his education. In the fall of 1893, he moved to Ann Arbor, Michigan, and enrolled in the University of Michigan's Graduate School Program in the College of Literature, Science, and the Arts. Miriam went with him.

Every week, Mary sent ten-dollar payments to Will for Miriam's care. By the end of October, Mary had sewn doll clothes, including undergarments, then a dress and cape, and finally a nightdress. In her diaries, Mary itemized the gifts she sent. For Christmas, 1893, Miriam received the new doll clothes along with a new doll. Mary also sent a souvenir spoon from the World's Fair as well as a handkerchief for Will. The day after Christmas, she noted her receipt of "letters and gifts from Miriam."

Mary and Will's affair-like relationship and the uncertainty of boarding Miriam overseas were over. As in previous years, Will was off at school and overseeing the care of their daughter. Mary must have known, at that time, that there was no future in their marriage.

Legal documents from a few years later reveal that Mary and Will divorced, but so far, no divorce records have been found. The divorce must have been as secretive as their marriage. Even the Congregational Church's doctrine was against them. It stated, "Marriage should be to us sacred, holy, for time, and for eternity. If disappointment, or suffering, or regret come, these are not causes, from Christ's standpoint, either for divorce or for a new attachment. Rather are they burdens to be borne until such time as the providence of God shall bond through death."

Ella Wheeler Wilcox's poems were published at the time in the *Ladies' Home Journal*. Mary altered a few words of Wilcox's poem *Winds of Fate* and copied it into her diary. The poem expressed the opposite directions of Mary and Will's lives. It read:

> One ship sails east and another west,
> With the very same winds that blow;
> 'tis the set of the sails and not the gales,
> That tell us the way to go.
> Like the winds of the sea
> Are the ways of fate,
> As we voyage along through life.
> 'tis the set of the soul that decides the goal,
> And not the calm or the strife.

PART 4
SEPARATE YEARS, 1893–1909

CHAPTER 21

THROUGHOUT THE HIDDEN YEARS OF MARY AND WILL'S ROMANCE AND marriage, Mary managed to keep her reputation unscathed. When she and two men were appointed to judge a Preparatory School contest, the editor of the Boulder *Daily Camera* wrote, "That settles it. No one could roast such a board as that."

Mary was continuously idolized by her students and former students. Two of them, Francis S. Kinder and F. Clarence Spencer, both of Denver, honored her with a book dedication. They had edited an anthology titled *Evenings with Colorado Poets*, and they wrote:

> To Our Friend and Former Instructor—Mary Rippon.
> The crowning pleasure in the compilation of this book
> is the privilege of dedicating it to you, and this
> token of personal esteem is not without special fitness,
> since to you we owe much of our love of the beautiful—
> a chief inspiration to the labor of our undertaking.

In the book were works from more than forty poets, both male and female. The first poem was by Helen Hunt Jackson, whose earlier writings on wildflowers had influenced Mary to come to Colorado.

As Mary continued her public academic life, Will and Miriam remained in the background. Mary still itemized the money she sent them and kept up her correspondence. Every year, on January 17, Mary continued to note "Miriam's day" in her diary. But, with the exception of the day Miriam was born, Mary never spent a birthday with her daughter.

In 1894, Miriam was five years old and living in Michigan with Will, who oversaw her care. With fewer distractions in her life and still healthy and active at the age of forty-four, Mary concentrated on her career. She collected interest on her loans and continued to pay the bills. The regents raised Mary's salary from fourteen hundred dollars to sixteen hundred dollars per year, even though the male professors made two thousand. The increase helped, but Miriam's expenses never ended, and Will had not paid back what he had borrowed.

Mary still lived with and paid room and board to the Bracketts. At the same time, she purchased a small farm as an investment. During a several-month period, she bought water shares and insurance and made repairs. After eight months, she sold the property for a modest profit. Then she paid off a debt to a friend and purchased four Boulder city lots. She borrowed money from one student and lent money to others, carefully noting payments, interest, and receipts in her account books. Loans ranged from as little as sixty-five dollars to as much as fourteen hundred dollars.

The Boulder Fortnightly and Delta Gamma clubs remained a large part of Mary's life. The Fortnightly Club had expanded from one room to two in the First National Bank Building in downtown Boulder. The rooms were carpeted and comfortably furnished with an oak table and bookcases. Delphine Bell had donated a matching oak armchair that the ladies called the "President's throne." Double shades and muslin curtains soothed tired eyes on sunny afternoons. Each member had her own key and could drop in any time to read or take home books. A stop at the club's rooms broke up the walk between the university and Mary's most recent room, at the Bracketts' home.

Little changed in Mary's life during the next year. From large gaps in her diary and a brief newspaper reference stating that she had gone out of town, it appears that Mary and Miriam may have vacationed together on Auntie's farm in Illinois. Miriam continued to call her mother "Aunt Mary." When Will finished his graduate studies in Michigan, he took Miriam with him and moved to Boston, Massachusetts. It is not known if he had been offered a job or why he chose to move there.

In February 1896, Mary confided to her diary that she had "house fever." Except for the first few months in Boulder in a hotel, she had

Figure 21.1. The Fortnightly Club met in two rooms over the First National Bank.

boarded in other people's homes for eighteen years. When the brick cottage next door to the Bracketts came up for sale, she decided it was time for a home of her own. The cottage was unpretentious and, according to her diary, suited her perfectly.

Mary made up her mind in two days. The location, at 2463 Twelfth Street, was north of the downtown area, but still within walking distance of the university, and just three blocks from her church. She took out a bank loan and wrote a check for the full price of seventeen hundred fifty dollars.

For three weeks, a carpenter worked on Mary's new home. He put a new floor in the front room and cut two doors. Mary then began wallpapering and painting. She gave away the chickens that came with the house and tore down the chicken coop in the back yard.

The Brackett family, with their son William, helped Mary move her few belongings. J. Raymond Brackett had by then become Dean of the College of Arts and Sciences. Everyone but Mary called him Dean

Brackett. Even though he was a close friend, she always referred to him as "Mr. Brackett" in her diaries. After her move, she still took her meals in their home.

Although she did not have to shop and cook, being a homeowner put demands on her time. During the next few months, when Mary was not teaching or meeting with students, she put up shades, acquired furniture, and arranged books and artwork. As the days got longer and the violets started to bloom near her back steps, she planted a flower garden of honeysuckle, pinks, tulips, hollyhocks, and clematis.

Shortly after Mary was settled in her new home, she received a letter from Will. He had fallen in love with a young woman, a twenty-four-year-old Connecticut girl named Dora Mae (Dorothy) Searles. At forty-six, Mary was old enough to have been her mother; Will was between them at age thirty-three. Their wedding was planned for the following summer.

Figure 21.2. After boarding with various families for eighteen years, Mary bought a home of her own.
PHOTO BY AUTHOR, 1995

In June 1896, Mary took a train to Boston, then rode out to the town of Plymouth on the shore. While she was there, Will married his new bride in a private family ceremony in New York City. The marriage license application, from the Borough of Manhattan, clearly states that the marriage was a second one for the groom. This proved that Will and Mary had to have gotten a divorce.

The day after the wedding, Will brought Miriam to Mary in Plymouth, and Mary cared for Miriam while Will and Dora Mae enjoyed their honeymoon. As mother and daughter picked up seashells and threw bits of bread to the seagulls, Mary may have felt like the "aunt" she claimed to be.

Will returned a few weeks later. His remarriage did not change his financial relationship with Mary. Although Miriam continued to live with Will, and then with Will and Dora Mae, Mary agreed to continue the child support. She either wanted to maintain control over their daughter, or Will was truly unable to financially provide for her. Or perhaps Mary was unwilling to let go of Will.

On Mary's way back to Colorado, she got off the train at Auntie's in Illinois. She stopped again in Topeka, Kansas, to visit her half-brother Omar Whitney. He had lived in Kansas ever since their mother, Jane, and Omar's father had left the Rippon farm in Lisbon Center, Illinois. Omar's son Norman (Mary's nephew) was the same age as Miriam. Just as the story of Mary's separate lives was passed down through the Bell and Brackett families, an interview with a Whitney family member confirmed that the story had filtered through that family, too.

The following Christmas, Mary noted in her diary that she sent Miriam a dress and Will fifty dollars. A few weeks later, on Miriam's eighth birthday, Will took her to a Boston photography studio and had her portrait taken. Miriam's brown eyes still flashed, but a slight sadness had crept into her expression. She may not have liked sharing Will with her new stepmother.

It is not known what Miriam was told at the time, if she asked why she did not have her own mother. She did, though, have contact with her paternal grandfather, Will's father Peter Housel—whose heirs would later find Miriam's eighth-birthday photograph among his possessions.

Figure 21.3. Miriam's portrait was taken on her eighth birthday while living in Boston with Will and his new wife.
AUTHOR'S COLLECTION

Mary was unable—or, perhaps, unwilling—to spend time with her family, filled her life with students and friends. Anna never visited from Germany, but she and Mary kept up a lively correspondence according to the lists of letters sent and received as noted in Mary's journals and diaries. Besides Lottie Brackett, next door, and of course Delphine Bell, Mary regularly visited with Lizzie Ellet, Helen Beardsley, and Caroline Greene. Lizzie was the widow of Mary's previous landlord, Helen had been the only other student in Will's graduating class, and Caroline lived just south of the Bracketts' home. On special occasions such as New Year's Day, these ladies and additional friends often gathered in Mary's home.

Mary was encouraged by her lady friends to give a second illustrated lecture on modern sculpture to the Fortnightly Club. A few months later, with additional lantern slides, she depicted the life and work of Italian painter Antonio Allegri da Correggio. Mary's photograph (Figure 21.4) was published in the December 17, 1899, Denver *Sunday Times* along with a lengthy article on the "Boulder Women and Their Club." At the time, Mary was first vice president, and membership was limited to thirty members.

In addition to researching serious topics, the club ladies also had lighter social meetings, such as a progressive conversational and guessing party held for one member who was moving away. A newspaper article titled "A Pretty Entertainment" stated that one lady's job was to ring a bell, signaling the rest of the ladies to answer a series of questions in order to advance to the next of nine tables. Topics included Browning, Shakespeare, popular quotations, characterization of authors, and characterization of club members.

Society still demanded that teachers be role models. The *Ladies Home Journal*, to which Mary subscribed, published an article titled "What It Means to Be a Teacher." The writer pointed out that a teacher, even more than a physician or clergyman, has the opportunity to uplift humanity. Teachers were expected to have the qualities of "profound reverence, strong and earnest faith, and complete consecration." Joseph Sewall would have agreed.

* * *

Figure 21.4. In 1899, Mary wore a fashionable dress with "leg-of-mutton" sleeves. A watch hung on a chain from the front of her dress.

As the nineteenth century neared an end, the student body at the university had increased to approximately five hundred and the faculty and staff to one hundred. Enrollment was no longer a problem, but the young institution had another financial crisis to endure, due to a failure in Colorado's revenues preventing the state legislature to meet appropriations for the university and other state institutions. University president James H. Baker assembled the student body and informed them that money was not available to pay professors or even to buy coal to heat the buildings. This time, Boulder citizens started an emergency fund solely to keep the doors open.

Mary went from door to door and called on several of the university's original subscribers, but she did not have much luck. Two of the donors had died, and their widows supported themselves by taking in washing. Mary donated two hundred fifty dollars of her own salary. Many of the other professors donated, as well.

In the summer of 1898, Mary met Dora Mae (Dorothy) for the first time. Will had moved his family to Buffalo, New York, where he applied for a position as a clerk with the United States Civil Service Commission. Mary stayed overnight in a hotel and then picked up nine-year-old Miriam for a visit to Illinois for the rest of the summer. By then, Will and his new wife had a new son, Roy Mandeville Housel.

The next year they had another son, James Robert Housel. If Miriam was unhappy before, she suddenly was forced to compete for attention with her half-brothers. Will was the only parent she thought she had.

The turmoil of Mary and Will's relationship appears to have ended with the separation of Mary's professional and private lives. She continued to teach German and to gain the respect of her students and colleagues. She made loans and investments in order to financially provide for her daughter. Mary was not the type to complain. If she thought her financial assistance was unfair, she may have rationalized it with duty and an increasing sense of guilt. After all, Will did provide Miriam with a home.

Ahead of them all was the beginning of a new century.

CHAPTER 22

By March 1900, Mary had saved up enough money for another European trip. She was forty-nine years old and had decided to treat herself to a viewing of the annual Easter Passion Play in the German village of Oberammergau in the Bavarian Alps. The last time she had been overseas was in 1891 when she had visited Will and Miriam in Geneva.

"On a vacation, Miss Mary Rippon is one of those people who does things without fuss and feathers," wrote a reporter for the *Boulder News*. "Last Thursday, she heard her classes at the University up to noon, graded the examination papers, and in the afternoon put on her hat and skipped out for Europe where she will remain until fall."

Mary had taught her German classes as usual during the fall and winter, then found instructors to fill in for her after spring vacation. She took a leave of absence, without pay, for the remainder of the school year.

After a stop to see her half-brother, Omar Whitney, in Topeka, she re-boarded the train. Her next stop was Chicago where Auntie had moved after remarrying and leaving the farm. The rural Illinois of her childhood became a blur from the train window. Her next train took her to Will's home in Buffalo, New York.

On March 29, Will recorded in his diary, "Mary came at 7:15 am." The next day he wrote "Mary took NYC [New York Central] train for NY at 1 pm." She had allowed herself only one day to visit with Miriam.

Although Mary still paid for Miriam's care, Will was weighted down with the responsibilities of his young family. He either did not get or did not accept the civil service job in Buffalo. Instead, he opened a business as a travel consultant, using his knowledge of overseas travel to book individuals on European tours.

Figure 22.1. Will lived in Buffalo, New York, when this photograph of him with his second-oldest son James was taken circa 1901.

AUTHOR'S COLLECTION

In New York, Mary boarded a ship for Rotterdam, Holland. Her only notation in her diary for the eleven-day crossing was "Stormy, remained in bed." She arrived in Hannover, Germany, on April 14 and wrote that Anna gave her "a warm welcome." Unlike her short visit with Miriam, Mary's visit with her old friend lasted for several weeks. Then Mary traveled to Munich, Germany, where she had arranged to meet Joseph Sewall's daughter Jennie and one of her friends. The three of them rode together on the train to Oberammergau.

The Passion Play lasted from eight o'clock in the morning to four o'clock in the afternoon and portrayed the life, death, and ascension of Christ. Four thousand people were in the audience. The only intermission was for lunch. Mary was particularly moved by the crucifixion scene, noting it in her diary as "almost unbearable."

Afterward, Mary returned to Hannover and stayed with Anna until the end of July. She then sailed out of Rotterdam in August. After another few days in New York, she again took a train to Buffalo. Will wrote in his diary that Mary brought them all gifts: an umbrella for Dorothy (Dora Mae), hairbrushes for himself and for Miriam, and chocolates for the little boys. This time, Mary stayed for two days and took eleven-year-old Miriam shopping.

Once Mary's classes were underway again in the fall, she prepared an illustrated lecture on the Passion Play and presented it to a packed audience at the Congregational Church. So many people came that she agreed to a second showing. A *Boulder County Herald* reporter wrote, "If the attendance of a large crowd is evidence of popularity, then surely Miss Rippon of the University is popular." At her home, a constant stream of students and former students gathered in her living room for evenings of stimulating conversation.

Will's travel business, meanwhile, had not been successful. In the summer of 1901, he moved his family to Ann Arbor, Michigan. He and his wife became the parents of another boy, Edgar Searles Housel.

While students and colleagues in Boulder assumed Mary was in Chicago, she, too, traveled on to Ann Arbor. According to her account book, she arrived just in time to buy baby Edgar what was called an "infant's incubator." Then she paid a twelve-dollar doctor's bill, spent four dollars for medicine, and took Miriam to the dentist. Will still needed her regular checks, but suddenly, with the latest baby, the payments were not enough. Will had been financially dependent on Mary ever since Miriam's birth, but Mary was still dependent on him to raise her.

In hopes of improving his situation, Will decided to go back into farming. He had learned the occupation from his father, and the business was one he thought he knew how to run. It is not known if he considered moving to his father's farm in Boulder, but the presence of twelve-year-old Miriam might have been too difficult to explain to friends of the family. Instead, Will chose an eighty-acre farm in Pittsfield Township, just south of Ann Arbor. There was only one problem—he did not have the money to buy it.

There was only one way for Mary to ensure that Miriam had a home, and that was for Mary to buy the farm herself. The price was three thousand four hundred dollars, more than two years of her annual salary. She arranged for semi-annual payments of three hundred dollars at five percent interest. Mary wrote in her account book that she made the first payment in April 1902. According to the property records, the deed was recorded under Mary's name. Finally, Will's occupation fit the word "Harvest"—his pseudonym in the secret telegraphic code that he had kept years before with Mary.

Mary wrote in her diary that she spent the summer of 1902 traveling back and forth between her friends in Detroit and the farm in Ann Arbor. She continued to buy necessities for the family. She purchased furniture for the house as well as fence posts, paint, lumber, a pump, shingles, and livestock feed. She also paid the property taxes and bought medicine, dry goods, and groceries. She even gave Dora Mae a few dollars of spending money.

Somehow, Mary had taken on the burdens of Will's entire family. In addition, she carried the mortgage on the home of her half-brother, Omar Whitney. Her own properties included her home in Boulder, a timber claim in northern Colorado, and some rental properties she had recently acquired in the states of Utah and Washington. She still made loans to students, sometimes securing the loans with life insurance policies.

In 1902, Mary remained the only female professor at the University of Colorado. Delphine Bell, who had taken over as an instructor for her French classes, had retired, but her twenty-three-year-old daughter Rosetta had just been appointed as an assistant instructor in Romance languages.

The next year, according to regents' minutes, male professors got a raise. Mary's salary, for reasons unknown, temporarily decreased. Society's reasoning had not changed since the Civil War. A single woman had only herself to support, while men were expected to support whole families. Little did the regents know that Mary provided for herself and a family of six.

CHAPTER 23

MARY'S DUAL OBLIGATIONS TUGGED AND PULLED AT HER PRIVATE AND public lives. She regularly sent money to Michigan while her public allegiance was directed toward the university.

In November 1902, the University of Colorado celebrated its twenty-fifth anniversary with a quarto-centennial celebration. Students and alumni participated in a parade that visually depicted a quarter-century of changes. No one knew more about them than Mary. The first graduating class, from 1882, was represented by students in a horse-drawn stagecoach. The senior class of 1903 waved from an automobile— one of the few in Boulder.

By the time of the quarto-centennial, the old cattle fence and stile had been gone for years, and trees surrounded Old Main. The campus included the President's House, the two dormitory cottages, Hale Scientific Building, Woodbury Hall, and seven other buildings. The library in Old Main outgrew its space, and a foundation had been laid for a separate library building.

The early buildings on the university campus comprised a mixture of architectural styles. Old Main and the President's House were of brick, while Hale and Woodbury were of stone. All faced north toward Boulder. Silver maples thrived along the walkway from Twelfth Street (now Broadway) over University (now Varsity) Pond to Old Main. An expanded curriculum included a College of Liberal Arts, a School of Applied Science, a School of Medicine, and a School of Law.

Mary finally had a colleague with whom to share the responsibility for protecting the morals of her female students. Former Dean of Wellesley College, Miss Margaret Stratton, became the University of

Figure 23.1. By 1903, trees surrounded Old Main, and the ravine had been turned into University Pond.
AUTHOR'S COLLECTION

Colorado's first official Dean of Women. She also served as an assistant English literature professor. By then there were more than two hundred fifty women on campus. Miss Stratton lived with the women in one of the dormitory cottages. Her duties included overseeing their intellectual, social, religious, and physical well-being. Although she answered their questions about what to wear to which social functions, she also did her share of spying on unchaperoned parties. When they needed a sympathetic ear or someone to listen to their problems, the young ladies still went to Mary.

At the end of the 1902–1903 academic year, the senior class dedicated its yearbook to Mary. Class members wrote:

> To her whom we love, as Friend and Teacher,
> Mary Rippon, this book is respectfully dedicated.

In September 1904, the Boulder *Daily Camera* published an article titled "She Mustn't Love." It was about a Boulder primary school teacher who, as Mary had done, secretly married "for fear the rule against married women teachers would be enforced." According to the article, when the school children "overheard the love ditties" and "saw the soft glow gathering in her eyes," the teacher's secret was revealed and she was forced to resign.

The newspaper's editor questioned the teacher's resignation by asking, "Is it to be inferred because a woman teacher is in love that she can't go through the year without being married? Or does the master passion so sap their energies and absorb the mind and weaken the firmness with which the birch should be handled as to render the victim incapable?"

By April 1905, Will was still in financial difficulties. Mary took out a new note and mortgage on his farm. The very same day, his eighty-one-year-old father, Peter Housel, died of "old age" following a short illness. Housel's obituary stated that he had "Gone Over the Range." He was praised as a Boulder pioneer, judge, miner, and farm owner who possessed a very large estate. Along with his sister and two brothers, "Will Housel of Ann Arbor, Michigan" was listed as an heir. It may have been Will's intention to repay his debts with his expected inheritance.

The following summer, Mary again traveled to Michigan and assisted the whole family, even buying clothes for the boys. Miriam was then sixteen years old and attending Ann Arbor High School. Perhaps because of Mary's love of music when she was a teenager, she enrolled Miriam in violin lessons.

It is not known what happened to the expensive piano purchased with Mary's trust fund when she lived with Uncle and Auntie in Lisbon Center. Since she boarded in other people's homes for the first eighteen years she lived in Boulder, the piano must have stayed behind in Illinois. Two months before Mary made the first payment on Will's farm, she bought herself another piano. It cost one hundred fifty dollars, equivalent to more than five thousand dollars today. But then, in the fall of 1905, she needed the money and sold the piano for the same amount.

In January 1906, after Miriam's seventeenth birthday, Mary took her on a trip to Europe—Miriam's first time overseas since arriving in the United States as a four-year-old. Again, as in 1900, Mary left the university during spring vacation. Delphine agreed to take over her German classes for the remainder of the school year. When Mary arrived in Ann Arbor, Dora Mae was expecting another child.

Mary and Miriam sailed from Portland, Maine, to Liverpool, England. Then they traveled on to Anna's home in Hannover. Mary and Anna each had their photograph taken in the same Hannover portrait studio. Both women wore their hair pulled back, had on long dark dresses, and looked somewhat matronly.

As Mary had done so many years earlier, she left Miriam overseas and returned to Boulder to teach. This time Mary left her, and money for her care, with Anna in Germany.

When Mary arrived home, she learned that Peter Housel had *not* left a will. An executor had spent more than two years settling his affairs for his "very large estate," which consisted of three farms in Boulder County and three properties within the city of Boulder. All but one property turned out to be encumbered. After his widow, Louisa, had paid off his debts, there was nothing left for Will or his siblings. The final account stated, "no balance to be distributed between the heirs." Even if Will had wanted to, he could not repay his debts to Mary.

In May 1907, Mary paid off Will's mortgage. Eventually she had the title conveyed from "Mary Rippon to William C. Housel." The house, barn, outbuildings, and eighty acres had not increased in value. By then Miriam had returned from Europe. Expenses for the family, now totaling seven, were even higher. The boys were nine, eight, and six years old. The youngest was baby Dorothy, then just a year old.

The next time Mary visited, she noted in her account book that she bought groceries, meat, dry goods, and shoes, paid an outstanding doctor bill, a three-month telephone bill, and a fifty dollar bill for a live-in nurse for two weeks. There were more farm expenses, too, including pig feed, fencing, hardware, lumber, paint, machine parts, and even a silo and a barn. Her money went into improving the real estate, just as her

Figure 23.2. Mary had this portrait taken on her 1906 trip to Germany. She was fifty-six at the time.
CARNEGIE LIBRARY FOR LOCAL HISTORY/MUSEUM OF BOULDER COLLECTION

Figure 23.3. Anna von Brandis, Mary's longtime friend from her student days, posed in the same photography studio.

inheritance had done when building the home and outbuildings for her mother and stepfather in Lisbon Center.

That fall, the regents restored Mary's salary from before the pay cuts, but financially she came up short. Instead of selling additional assets, as she had done with the piano, she took out an eight-hundred-dollar loan, with interest, from her friend and neighbor Lottie Brackett. Mary carefully noted her payments throughout the year it took her to pay off the bills for Will and his family.

Meanwhile, Mary's students placed her on a pedestal. Under her photograph in the yearbook, they wrote: "Earth's noblest thing—a woman perfected."

Mary's separate lives could not have been further apart.

CHAPTER 24

By the spring of 1909, Mary's bouts of neuralgia and respiratory problems sometimes kept her at home. On her better days, she still managed to teach her German classes in Old Main. Twelfth Street (now Broadway) had become congested with a busy mixture of automobiles, bicycles, and horse-drawn carriages and wagons. Mary was grateful for the streetcar that now stopped in front of her home and eliminated the long walk up the hill to the university.

The streetcar route passed the new Congregational Church. Its membership had outgrown the small brick building on the north side of Pine Street, so the old church was torn down and replaced with a larger one across the street.

One block beyond the church was the beginning of Boulder's commercial district. The streets were either dusty or muddy depending upon the weather, but solid flagstone sidewalks had replaced the old wooden ones. On the corner of Twelfth and Spruce streets, prohibitionists had erected the Willard Building, named for Frances Willard, the past national president of the Women's Christian Temperance Union.

On the east side of the intersection of Pearl and Twelfth streets was the First National Bank building (later, in 1921, replaced with a new bank building) where the Fortnightly and Delta Gamma clubs met. Downstairs, next to the bank lobby, was the depot for the Interurban railroad to Denver. The electrically powered railroad cars made sixteen round-trips to Denver every day.

Valentine's Hardware store was in the brick Boettcher Building on the west side of the intersection. The building dated from 1878, the same year that Mary arrived in Boulder. Gold mining had continued in Gold

Hill, Ward, and other mountain towns, while silver strikes in Caribou also boosted the county's economy. In Boulder, Valentine's was the place where miners went for supplies. The miners and their wives or sweethearts held dances every Saturday night in the big hall upstairs.

After another two blocks, the streetcar crossed Boulder Creek and climbed the hill to the university. Mary got off at the President's House, then occupied by President James Baker and his family. Mature trees and green lawns replaced the sagebrush and rocky soil of the early years. On University Hill, to the west, neatly laid-out avenues and stately homes covered the previously wild and unkempt prairie. Within the preceding few years, people in Boulder had begun comparing the rock faces on the mountainsides with clothes irons on end, their flat surfaces facing outward. Soon the mountains became known as the "flatirons."

The fragrance of the plum thicket mingled with that of the apple blossoms and lilacs. A stone bridge led over University Pond, and the campus had continued to grow. The Guggenheim Law building was under construction next to the completed Buckingham Library. These new buildings did not face Boulder, like the earlier ones, but instead were spaced around a large grassy area called the Quadrangle.

At the age of fifty-nine, Mary walked slowly and found it harder and harder to climb the steep steps of Old Main. Delphine's daughter Rosetta assisted Mary in her German classes. Rosetta had grown into a beautiful young woman, had studied in Europe, and had married Charles Wolcott, one of the sons of Will's father's widow, Louisa. Rosetta had been a ten-year-old child when Mary visited the Bell family in Geneva a few months after Miriam was born. Rosetta had grown up knowing of Mary's separate lives.

Toward the end of the school year, Rosetta kept a diary and commented that Mary looked quite ill. In later correspondence between Mary and Rosetta, Mary stated that she could not have finished the semester without her.

The emotional and financial demands from Mary's public and private lives drained her health and sapped her energy. While she continued to share her enthusiasm for German literature and "mothered" her students, she probably worried silently about Miriam's education and her future.

Upon learning of the new retirement fund established by an endowment from industrialist and philanthropist Andrew Carnegie, Mary decided it was time to retire. The Carnegie Foundation for the Advancement of Teaching provided pensions for teachers of nonsectarian institutions of higher learning in the United States and Canada. Its only requirement was twenty-five years of continuous service. Mary's association with the university spanned more than thirty years.

In Mary's application to the Carnegie Foundation, she listed her years of teaching and added that she had "spent two years and several shorter vacations in study abroad." Briefly she mentioned her five years of initial studies in Germany, Switzerland, and France, but still there was no mention of her ever having received a degree.

In 1909, students, reluctant to see her go, again dedicated their yearbook to Mary. They wrote:

> Who sees thy face sees kindness, lord of all
> And that the soul is there, behind thine eyes
> Is surety and faith and not surmise;
> A soul to help and aid what e'er befall.
> A soul to harken to each earnest call,
> To save from folly; make us truly wise
> As thou art; give to us a humble guise
> To stand before thee in thy learning's hall;
> As oft before, in our simplicity
> We ask thee to vouchsafe a greater light
> To teach our falt'ring erring eyes to see,
> Our ears to hear thy precepts—learn aright:
> We learn from thee the law of gentleness,
> And with the others gone, thy name to bless.

After Mary's retirement, the regents decided they wanted a woman to take her place. Even though she was ill, Mary agreed to aid them in their search. As soon as the 1908–1909 academic year was over, she wrote for advice to Calvin Thomas, professor of Germanic languages and literature at Columbia University in New York.

Mary described the type of woman she hoped to find. All of the qualities except the doctoral degree were ones that she herself possessed. Professor Thomas's response was preserved with Mary's diaries. The letter read:

Dear Madam, I have delayed answering your letter of June 6 in the hope that I might get some valuable light on your problem—in other words, discover the person you want, but I have had no success. You are probably aware that the combination of attractive qualifications which you describe—

a. A PhD
b. An experienced teacher
c. A person who has been in Germany
d. A person who can give instruction to graduate students
e. A woman of admirable appearance and personality
f. A model of fine spirit and enthusiasm for scholarship and character—is rare almost to the point of unearthliness. I hope you may be able to locate your paragon, but up to date I am powerless to help you.

Sincerely, Calvin Thomas

PART 5

RETIREMENT YEARS, 1909–1935

CHAPTER 25

THE PHOTOGRAPH OF MARY TAKEN ON HER PREVIOUS TRIP TO GERmany made the front page of the Boulder *Daily* Camera in July 1909. Underneath was the caption "Loved teacher of German and Literature who is to benefit by Carnegie Foundation." In the accompanying article, titled "Miss Rippon Resigns After Long Service," a reporter wrote, "Her successor has not as yet been chosen. Miss Rippon's unremitting labors have rendered her ill and she is spending the summer in bed at her home on Twelfth Street. A more lovable personality and teacher cannot be found in any institution of learning."

The university publication *Silver and Gold* echoed these sentiments by stating, "The long years of continued service brought on ill health which was the cause of her resignation . . . By her untiring energy as a teacher and her lovable personality, she has brought the German Department to its present high standing and popularity, and all who knew her will be sorry to learn of her departure from the University."

A worsening of Mary's physical ailments may have brought on her illness, or she may have had a nervous breakdown resulting from the mental strain and exhaustion of her two separate lives. For two decades, she had managed to hide her marriage and child from everyone in Boulder except Delphine and her family, the Bracketts, and Will's father, Peter Housel.

Throughout the summer, Mary continued a letter-writing campaign in an effort to locate her replacement. Eventually she found Miss Grace Fleming van Sweringen, an 1893 graduate from Cornell University who had earned a Doctor of Philosophy degree from the University of Berlin. In an interview, years later, Mary stated, "Her letters of recommendation were among the best I had ever seen. I knew she would make a fine success of the work I loved so well."

Finally, the day-to-day responsibilities of Mary's professional life were over, but supporting twenty-year-old Miriam would continue. At the time, Miriam was living with Will while attending the University of Michigan, also in Ann Arbor. Then, for reasons unknown, Miriam rebelled. Mary's diary entry simply stated, "M. left the farm August 10, 1909." On August 26, Mary felt well enough to board a train. She met Miriam at the Pratt Hotel in Frankfort, Michigan, a small town on the eastern shore of Lake Michigan.

Miriam did not want to return to the farm. Instead, she and Mary took a lake steamer and then a train to Madison, Wisconsin. There Mary enrolled her in the University of Wisconsin's Department of Letters and Science at the beginning of the 1909–1910 academic year.

According to Mary's diary, Mary rented a house in Madison where they both lived. Mary still paid Miriam's expenses, but she had to spend her money wisely, as her pension provided her with only eighty percent of her previous salary. Still, there were beds and additional furniture to purchase, as well as groceries, clothing, and books.

Mary had not fully recovered from her illness, but she found relaxing ways to pass her time. She rented a piano. She also attended services of the local Congregational Church. In March 1910, she wrote a letter to Rosetta Bell and confided:

> It has taken me a long time to gain any degree of strength, but it is coming little by little. I can endure no excitement and have none. My life here is extremely quiet and regular. I am not in the least despondent or restless—am happy and quite willing to be as idle as the law allows.

A month later, Mary took a train from Madison to Chicago and then went on to Ann Arbor to visit Will. Her continued pattern of summer visits may have been one of the rituals of their relationship, just like the Sunday visits Will had made years before in Boulder. They may have discussed Will's desire to sell the farm, as he was interested, at the time, in starting a coal-selling business. Even though Mary had transferred the property deed into Will's name, it was her money that paid for it.

After her visit in Michigan, Mary returned to her home in Boulder.

Miriam, meanwhile, had enrolled in a German literature class. She later claimed to have been swept off her feet by her handsome young instructor, a German-born student assistant named Rudolf Rieder just three years her senior. In 1889, at the age of three, Rudolf had immigrated to America with his parents who settled in Milwaukee and became naturalized American citizens.

A few months after meeting her new instructor, Miriam discovered she was pregnant. She and Rudolf quietly married. The next month, she dropped out of school while he continued his undergraduate studies and student teaching. In November 1910, Mary sent the newlyweds two hundred dollars as a wedding gift and noted the expenditure in her diary.

By the spring of 1911, Mary had finally regained her health. She embarked on a trip to the west coast and stayed with friends in Long Beach and San Diego, California. There she spent her time knitting, crocheting, and, again, playing the piano.

Mary was in Los Angeles when she received word that on April 25, Miriam had given birth to a son named Walfried Wolf Rieder. At the time, Rudolf was employed as a teacher and was earning five hundred dollars per year, equivalent to more than sixteen thousand dollars in today's currency. Mary immediately took a train to Boulder where she went to her bank and sent them more money. Then she took the train to Topeka to see her half-brother, Omar Whitney. She also bought baby clothes and visited Auntie in Chicago. Always practical, Mary even noted in her account book that she purchased not one but two life insurance policies for Rudolf, the new father.

While Miriam and her family were getting settled, Mary and Will continued their correspondence as grandparents. In April 1912, Will's wife Dora Mae, who was then thirty-nine, became ill. She died five weeks later. Funeral services were held at the family's home before her burial in Ann Arbor's Forest Hill Cemetery.

During this crisis in Will's life there was nothing Mary could do. Instead of rushing to his side, she boarded a Red Star liner in

Philadelphia and sailed to Antwerp, Belgium. The trip was her eighth sea crossing. Mary had become a seasoned traveler, but she may have been nervous. Just a few weeks before she left, the White Star Line's RMS *Titanic* had sunk on her maiden voyage.

Rudolf, Miriam, and baby Walfried joined Mary in Germany a few months later. Rudolf had completed his bachelor's degree in German and French at the University of Wisconsin. The family were staying together at a hotel in Munich when Miriam received a telegram that notified her of her father's death. On October 4, 1912, Will had been killed in a traffic accident. When the mail reached them, Mary, Miriam, and Rudolf learned that Will had been riding a motorcycle and was hit by a truck driven by the superintendent of the Eastern Michigan Edison Company. According to a newspaper article, the truck skidded, spun completely around, struck a curb and a telephone pole, and then turned nearly upside down. Surprisingly, the driver was not seriously injured. Will had been thrown from his motorcycle and was carried unconscious to a nearby house. An ambulance took him to a hospital where he died of a fractured skull.

An inquest was held to determine the cause of the accident. The coroner stated that Will was at fault by making an inappropriate turn. The accident was called "unavoidable," and the driver exonerated. Will was four days short of his fiftieth birthday.

Will's four orphaned children—fourteen-year-old Roy, thirteen-year-old James, eleven-year-old Edgar, and six-year-old Dorothy—again sat through a parent's funeral in their home. Will was buried beside his young wife in the Forest Hill Cemetery. His headstone matched hers.

Tragedy struck again a few months later when little Dorothy died of double pneumonia. Within one year, Will's second family of six had been reduced to just the three boys: Roy, James, and Edgar.

It was unlikely that Miriam knew even then that Mary had ever been married to Will or that she was anyone but her "Aunt Mary." After Will's death, Mary probably felt the need to be alone. She traveled through Belgium, Germany, France, Italy, and Switzerland and immersed herself in beauty and culture. If her trip was like her previous ones, she spent long hours in art museums, attended concerts and plays, and walked among the wildflowers.

Just three years after the end of her professional career, Mary was suddenly faced with the end of her friendship with Will. He may have been the only man she had ever loved. She copied into her diary James Whitcomb Riley's poem "He Is Not Dead." It read:

I cannot say and I will not say,
He is dead. He is just away.
With a cheery smile and a wave of the hand,
He has wandered into an unknown land,
And we are dreaming how very fair
It needs must be, since he lingers there.

Figure 25.1. Will is buried with his second wife and his daughter Dorothy in the Forest Hill Cemetery in Ann Arbor, Michigan.
AUTHOR'S COLLECTION

Chapter 26

Despite the pain of her loss, Will's death marked the beginning of a less turbulent time in Mary's life. The ups and downs that Mary had experienced were defined by her eight European journeys. First was the study class with Mrs. L. N. Stone that evolved into Mary's five-year university education and her friendship with Anna. Then, in 1883, after Mary had established her professional career at the University of Colorado, she took a year's sabbatical in which she "tried to decide future plans and failed." She then was thirty-three years old, admitted to being lonely, was about to lie about her age, and may have felt that she had ignored the womanly side of her life.

Mary's third ocean journey marked the beginning of her hidden—and then her separate—lives. On the 1888 trip, she traveled to Germany to deliver her baby. The next two trips were in the summers of 1890 and 1891 to visit Will and little Miriam.

When Mary left Boulder in 1900 for the Passion Play in Oberammergau, her double life had settled down. For the first time, she lived in her own home. And with Will's remarriage, Miriam had a home as well. Six years later, when Mary took it upon herself to teach Miriam firsthand about European culture, Mary had weathered her roughest financial years by easing Will through his several financial crises.

Mary's last European trip came after she had finally recovered from her lengthy exhaustion and illness, only to be hit with the sudden news of Will's death. When she arrived back in Boulder in 1913, she was still "aunt" to her daughter and "mother" to her former students, but Miriam was an adult with a child of her own, and the students visited as old friends.

Mary appeared to have put the past behind her, and she graciously accepted the continued recognition of her friends and colleagues. Mary's home became an informal international center as a constant stream of former German- and French-speaking students held lively discussions of world events. She decorated her rooms with books and souvenirs from her travels.

At the university, the maples between the President's House and Old Main had matured into shade trees. In the fall, they turned brilliant shades of red and gold, while yellow aspens in the mountains reached their height of glory. At least one year, in September, Mary took the narrow-gauge Denver, Boulder & Western railroad to the town of Ward and rented a cabin for a week. By then she was in her sixties and grateful for the return of her health.

After the end of winter, Mary carefully cultivated the flowers that grew in her garden. She noted in her diary the dates that she gave away bunches of delicately beautiful and fragrant lilies of the valley. She and her friend Delphine occasionally packed picnic suppers and ate them together at Boulder's Red Rocks, now a city of Boulder park.

There, with the mountains behind them, they could look out over the city that, by then, had topped nine thousand in population. Boulder spread from Chautauqua Park on the south, to the large homes of Mapleton Hill and newer residential areas farther north. From their vantage point, the university campus was no longer a barren bluff but rather a collection of buildings in a forest of trees. Beyond were farmlands that stretched to the eastern horizon.

Mary remained active in the Boulder Fortnightly Club and still attended the Congregational Church. She also attended the Scientific Society lectures at the university, especially when her neighbor and friend J. Raymond Brackett was the speaker. Mary still enjoyed visiting the Bracketts in their home. She described these visits in a letter to a former student:

> In the evening I often read aloud to the two who recline on the two couches in the sitting room—or as Dr. [J. Raymond] Brackett calls it "the sleeping car." Just now we are on the fourth volume of O'Henry's

stories. They are great fun, and the greatest fun is to see Dr. B shake when there comes an unexpected turn or expression. If you need medicine of this sort try "The Heart of the West." Perhaps you have.

After Will's death, Miriam and Rudolf stayed in Germany for another year. While Rudolf began his graduate work, Miriam cared for baby Walfried and may also have taken some classes. Many years later, Walfried (renamed Wilfred) wrote in an introduction to a collection of manuscripts of Miriam's that his parents' marriage "had been a tempestuous one." He added, "Two strong personalities clashed, and considerable time was spent in separations. Perhaps the happiest time they had was the two years they spent in study in pre-war Germany."

All this was expensive. Mary continued to send Miriam money. By then, Mary must have sold some of her properties as there was no other way that, given her small retirement income, she could have come up with the funds. At the end of 1912, she summarized her expenses and realized she had given Miriam more than twelve hundred dollars during the previous year. The current equivalent would be more than thirty-eight thousand dollars. Mary recorded in her account book that she sent Miriam more money that year than she had spent on herself. Again, as she had done with Will, Dora Mae, and their children, Mary found herself supporting Miriam, her husband, and their child.

Miriam, Rudolf, and Walfried returned to Madison, Wisconsin, before December 1913. At that time, Miriam sent Christmas gifts from Madison to her half-brothers in Ann Arbor, Michigan. Her letter was friendly and signed "Lots of love to all of you." The goodwill stopped abruptly the next year with the administration of Will's estate.

Will, like his own father, and Mary's too, had died intestate. Most of Will's property, again like his father's, was encumbered. In 1914, the Washtenaw County, Michigan, court declared that Roy, James, and their brother Edgar were sole heirs-at-law. Each boy received an inheritance of approximately one hundred thirty dollars: one-third each of Will's known real and personal estate. Miriam was not even acknowledged.

In the fall of 1914, Rudolf accepted a teaching position at the University of Washington in Seattle. Miriam took the opportunity to continue her undergraduate education. She had accumulated enough credits at the universities of Michigan and Wisconsin to enter, as a senior, the College of Liberal Arts at the University of Washington. According to the University's records, she took courses in French, Italian, and German. Miriam and Rudolf must have shared caring for Walfried. "Mrs. Miriam E. Rieder" received her Bachelor of Arts degree in French in June 1915.

After Miriam's graduation, the family returned to Madison, where Rudolf again taught German. Shortly afterward, Miriam became quite ill, according to her son's later writings. She was five feet six inches tall and normally a little plump. Then her weight dropped to only ninety-seven pounds.

In the summer of 1916, Mary was invited to house-sit in New Haven, Connecticut. The Bracketts' son William had bought a home there with his bride Rose and needed someone to care for the house while they were out of town. Meanwhile, Miriam (somewhat recovered), Walfried, and Rudolf had steamship tickets to travel to Sweden, where Rudolf had been asked to translate a book. In order to accommodate his college schedule, he had planned the trip for late fall or early winter.

Miriam wrote in her passport application that she was concerned about Walfried's safety and wanted to travel earlier in the fall in order to avoid the later stormy season at sea. She hoped to visit Anna in Germany but changed her plans when she heard that many German civilians were dying in an influenza epidemic. Luckily Anna and her family had been spared, but Miriam, still severely underweight, did not want to take any chances with her or her son's health. In early September, Miriam and Walfried left New York on a new Scandinavian-American liner. Mary was at the pier to see them off. According to her diary, she tucked one hundred seventy dollars into their traveling bag.

Miriam and Walfried arrived in a Europe that was at war, so Miriam decided to wait for Rudolf in the small village of Melano on the shore of Lake Lugano in the Italian-speaking section of Switzerland. There she expanded her knowledge of Italian. At first, the thin American woman who also spoke English, French, and German was considered suspicious by the town's tight-knit community, but gradually she and Walfried became accepted.

Miriam and her five-year-old son moved into a small villa on the lower portion of Mount San Generoso. There was little tourism because of the war, so rents were low and the little family was able to live frugally. Miriam's only source of income were bank drafts that Mary sent to her through the Swiss Consulate. In her unpublished memoirs, Miriam wrote that often all she could afford was a small skein of wool to darn Walfried's socks, yet she tried to make their time there as pleasant for him as she could. That first Christmas she bought a tiny tree and trimmed it with bits of chocolate wrapped in tinsel paper, then finished it with Jerusalem and holly berries gathered in the woods.

Mother and son waited patiently, but Rudolf never came. In 1917, the United States became involved in the Great War, and Rudolf's passport was denied because of his involvement in a German political group in Wisconsin. His perceived sympathies lay on the side of the Germans.

To help American soldiers overseas, Mary sold her timber claim near Walden, Colorado, then invested the six hundred dollars she received in half a dozen hundred-dollar Liberty bonds. She noted in her diary that on Christmas Eve 1917, she started knitting a sweater to be sent to any American soldier who needed it. She finished the sweater two weeks later and donated it, along with several pairs of hand-knitted socks, to the Red Cross that had set up headquarters in the Hotel Boulderado, in Boulder, Colorado.

Meanwhile, Miriam and Walfried remained stuck on the other side of the ocean. Usually they received Mary's checks, and their letters managed to get through. In her memoirs, Miriam wrote that she wanted to come home, but she did not want to make the trip with Walfried as long as the waters were likely to be infested with German submarines. Apparently, the American Consul in Zurich had tried to order her to leave by refusing to renew her passport, but the Swiss government allowed her to remain with her old passport until the danger from the U-boats was over.

Like Mary, Miriam loved wildflowers. On a sunny day in May 1918, while Walfried was playing with friends in Melano, Miriam and a German woman searched for new flower varieties on the slopes of Mount

San Generoso behind her home. The farther they hiked uphill, the closer they came to the border between Switzerland and Italy. Miriam had seen the boundary marker on an earlier hike, but the sign had washed away in the previous spring thaw.

On this particular day, the usual Italian border guard was nowhere near his post. Without realizing where they were, the two women wandered into Italy. Then they were suddenly—and without warning—held at gunpoint, escorted down the other side of the mountain, accused of being spies, and thrown into prison.

Although Walfried was well cared for by the villagers, he later wrote (in the introduction to an unpublished manuscript by Miriam) that he cried himself to sleep that night while men from Melano searched the mountain trails with lanterns. No one knew what had become of the women until several days later when an Italian border guard came to town and started asking questions.

After four weeks of constant pleading and begging in Italian, Miriam managed to convince her captors to set them free. The women were taken back to Melano hungry and in their same dirty clothing but with a greater knowledge of the Italian language. In her memoirs, Miriam noted that she began a letter to Mary with the sentence, "I just got back from a very unpleasant sojourn in Italy."

Eventually, the American Consul issued Miriam a short-term extension to her passport. Then, finally, on November 11, 1918, the day the Armistice was signed, the weary mother and son boarded a ship to come home. The war was over, and the seas were calm once more.

The turmoil of the war and the early years of Miriam's marriage were in the past. Rudolf had remained in Madison and had received his doctoral degree in French and German the preceding August. Mary may have assumed that with all his years of education, Rudolf would finally be able to support his wife and child. Yet, like Will with his lengthy education, Rudolf did not. Instead, he and Miriam, then thirty years old, decided to separate. Rudolf moved to Germany and wanted Walfried to go with him. Miriam refused and Americanized Walfried's name to Wilfred. Mother and son moved to Colorado.

When Miriam wrote her memoirs, she stated that her "aunt" told her it was her duty to take up education as a profession—that it was time to devote herself to "the dissemination of knowledge and breadth of culture [she] had acquired at the expense of much time and large sums" of Mary's money.

CHAPTER 27

ONE BY ONE, PEOPLE IMPORTANT IN MARY'S LIFE PASSED AWAY. Eighty-six-year-old Dr. Sewall died in 1917, on Miriam's birthday. His funeral was held two days later in his Denver home. Mary must have been in attendance. Dr. Sewall had been her father figure, perhaps even the embodiment of her conscience. The funeral would have given Mary a chance to reflect on how Dr. Sewall influenced her life. Without his invitation to teach in Boulder, she probably would have completed her contract at Detroit High School. She could have moved on to teach in one of the women's schools in the East or accepted the position she was offered from the University of Illinois. Without Dr. Sewall, it would have been unlikely that she would have come to Colorado, where she met Will.

Will's stepmother, Louisa Housel, also died in 1917. She had lived with her son Charles Wolcott and his wife Rosetta and, in the family, was the last remaining member of her generation. Louisa was buried in Green Mountain Cemetery next to her husband, Peter Housel. On his other side is Will's mother, Eliza Housel—reinterred by her family from her previous grave in Columbia Cemetery.

In 1919, Miriam found her first teaching job at a public school in the small agricultural town of Hugo on Colorado's eastern plains. She lived with her then-eight-year-old son (whose name, by then, had been changed to Wilfred), and she taught French and Spanish during the school's 1919–1920 academic year. Miriam was quick to admit that she was not happy with the job, the meager nine-hundred-dollar annual salary, nor the location. In her memoirs, she wrote that the scenery was "arid and uninteresting." She called the landscape "entirely on the drab side."

Rudolf, by this time, had become involved with the National Socialist German Workers' Party in Germany. Miriam strongly disagreed with its political philosophy. When interviewed by a federal census worker in 1920, she lied about her German birthplace and said she was born in France.

After Miriam completed her year's contract, she and Wilfred moved to Boulder. Because of circumstances that later became apparent, it is believed that she still did not know Mary was her mother. Instead, Mary continued to act as a doting aunt, keeping her true relationship with Miriam a secret from everyone except Lottie and J. Raymond Brackett, Delphine Bell, and Delphine's daughter Rosetta Bell Wolcott.

Yet Mary and Miriam visited openly. Miriam applied for a job at the university and was accepted as an instructor of French, Italian, and Spanish in the Romance language department. Miriam's situation was much like Delphine's had been when she was widowed with children. Rosetta, who had assisted in Mary's classes, also became a Romance language instructor that same year. She, however, did have a husband and children. By the 1920s, mores had changed. Even so, Rosetta's position was unusual. At the time, a poll of school boards by the National Educational Association showed that half of the school systems in the country forced female teachers to resign if they married.

Miriam and Rosetta both had offices above the creaking stairs of Old Main. Often they worked together to prepare their classes, and they quickly became good friends. Since Miriam's grandfather, Peter Housel, had married Rosetta's husband's mother, Louisa Wolcott, they were in a sense related. Perhaps Rosetta's knowledge of Mary and Miriam's mother-daughter relationship made Mary realize that the time had come to explain to Miriam that she was really her mother.

The story Mary was said to have told Miriam was a face-saving untruth which, for a time, served as an explanation. It was passed on from Miriam to Ross Ingersoll, a trusted student of hers. As the story went, early in her teaching career, Mary had taken a year's sabbatical to study in Europe. She and Will met on the ship on the voyage overseas. They quickly fell in love and married when the ship reached Germany. By the time Miriam was born, Mary and Will knew the marriage would

Figure 27.1. Rosetta Bell Wolcott (left) and Miriam (right) taught Romance languages together. Photo in 1933.
AUTHOR'S COLLECTION

not work. Mary left Miriam in Will's care and returned to the university to teach.

This skimpy, romanticized version of Will and Mary's marriage must not have endeared Mary to Miriam, for she continued to refer to her mother as "Aunt Mary" the rest of her life. According to the author's correspondence with the late Ross Ingersoll, the women continued their ongoing "aunt-niece" friendship instead of starting over as a reunited mother and daughter.

Unlike Mary's students, Miriam had no real role models in her life. She must have felt rejected by both Mary and Will when they nearly abandoned her as a young child in Switzerland and France. According to Miriam's student Ross Ingersoll, Will was the parent she described in far more favorable terms. She never mentioned Will's second wife and family or the financial hardships she endured on the Michigan farm. Miriam implied bitterness toward her estranged husband Rudolf and said as little as possible about Mary.

Shortly after Miriam began her teaching career at the university, she dropped her Spanish classes in order to concentrate on French and Italian. She also studied and earned her master's degree in "Literary Sources of Italian Opera." Like Mary, Miriam had a love for European languages and cultures and passed on her enthusiasm to her students. They were devoted to her in return, but outside the classroom Miriam avoided close relationships and, at the time, she did not seem to trust anyone.

In Miriam's early years at the university, she and Wilfred moved into a house at 1801 South Broadway, later replaced by Wardenburg Student Health Center. Wilfred walked across and down the street to the University Hill Elementary School. Miriam was close enough to the university campus to hear Old Main's bell announce the beginning of each class.

According to one of her students, Miriam often worked in her garden and rushed to the classroom without stopping to change her clothes or even wash her hands. Everyone who knew her commented on her lack of interest in her appearance. Mary, however, always wore dresses, even in the garden, and kept her silvery-white hair neatly tied back in a knot. She never allowed any loose ends.

CHAPTER 28

No longer could Mary walk next door for a friendly discussion with fellow professor J. Raymond Brackett. In 1922, her friend and neighbor suffered a severe attack of influenza. He had lain in bed for fourteen weeks, then, at the age of sixty-eight, died of heart complications. Mary could only visit him in the northwest corner of Columbia Cemetery where his stone was erected near that of Delphine's husband, Dr. James Bell.

As Mary's circle of friends grew smaller, the praise for her past accomplishments grew larger. Two alumni members, the original compilers of an anthology, *Evenings With Colorado Poets*, reprinted their book and re-dedicated it to Mary. "High honor is paid a prominent and popular Boulder woman," wrote a Boulder *Daily Camera* reporter in 1926.

Mary was one of the newspaper's regular subscribers and, according to those who knew her, kept up with current events. Therefore, it was likely that she read the lead story on the front page, on January 27, 1927, in which university President George Norlin repudiated a "campus scandal."

Reginald Spaulding Sibbald, one of Miriam's fellow instructors in the Romance language department, was "unfavorably linked in gossip" with a female sophomore. After a thorough investigation by university officials of the charges and counter charges, no proof of a sexual relationship was found, and no action was taken. As a result of all the publicity, the student was said to be "ill."

By then, young women wore skirts to their knees and bobbed their hair. Mary, on the other hand, never left her home without her hat and gloves. She still went to church and club meetings and followed the events at the university. In November 1927, the university celebrated its fiftieth anniversary. In another newspaper article Mary was acknowledged as the only living member of the early faculty and was recognized for the outstanding part she played "in her quiet modest way."

She attended all three days of the Semi-Centennial Program held in the spacious new Macky Auditorium. President Norlin gave an introductory address that was followed by a speech from Bishop Charles Mead of the Methodist Church. Reminiscent of Dr. Sewall, he spoke of an atmosphere in which good flourishes and evil disappears and stated, "All institutions must be judged by whether they exalt human life or not."

As an honored alumna, Mary was interviewed for *Colorado Alumnus* magazine in 1928. The reporter stated, "It fell to Miss Rippon to be a pioneer in college education in Colorado and to be one of the first women to gain a place on the faculty of an institution with university ambitions."

After an explanation of the warning Mary had received so many years earlier from the minister who visited Boulder and deemed the university's only building unsafe, Mary was quoted as saying, "I have never regretted my move, and Old Main has survived. I enjoyed every minute of my teaching experiences at the University and other associations with the institution. I desire to remain near the University that I may further watch its development and to remain in Boulder, which was in '79 [*sic*], as it is now, one of the most beautifully situated cities in the world." (Mary arrived in Boulder in 1878.)

In describing Mary, the writer continued, "Though she shares the pride of others identified with the University in its development, its growth, and in the high ranking it has gained in the educational world, Miss Rippon's greatest source of pleasure comes from the friendships that she made and in the successes that have been achieved by the men and women that she taught or who were in school during the years that she was on the faculty."

One of Mary's earliest students, Timothy Stanton, became a paleontologist for the United States Geological Survey. Ernest Pease, who was so interested in her descriptions of paintings when he visited her in Paris, became a Latin professor at Stanford University.

Miriam and Wilfred mixed in with the steady stream of former students who visited their revered professor in her Twelfth Street home. Mary's nephew Norman Whitney and his family came too. Norman was the son of her late half-brother Omar whom she had often visited in Topeka. Norman was a machinist for the Santa Fe Railroad and earned free railroad passes that he used to take his wife and children to Boulder to see Mary. Norman's ten-year-old daughter Joy always enjoyed those visits. In an interview with the author, she stated, "Our conversations turned to current events and to what I was learning at school. When I went off to college, she insisted on paying for my first year."

At the time, the railroads had lost much of their business to people who drove their own automobiles. Mary had never learned to drive, but her account book shows that she purchased a 1925 Chevrolet for Miriam to use to take her on outings.

Meanwhile, Will's sons still lived in Ann Arbor, Michigan. Roy, the oldest, had become proprietor of the Blue Front Cigar Store. Mary had assisted in the building's purchase while Will was still alive. More than a decade had passed since the probate of his estate. Since the store property was not in Will's name, but in Mary's, it had not been included in the settlement.

One day, Miriam approached Mary with a copy of a title insurance policy she had received from the Washtenaw Abstract Company in Ann Arbor. Her half-siblings had put the cigar store up for sale. In the document, the Housel brothers agreed to indemnify the abstract company from any loss that could arise on account of any interest Miriam may have retained in the property. The abstract company stated it was "fearful" that Miriam may have an undivided interest in the property.

Miriam, as one of Will's children, was entitled to her share. In order to file her claim, she needed proof of her parentage. During the research for this book's first edition, a Housel family member discovered a letter Miriam wrote, in March 1927, to the Recorder of Deeds in St. Louis, Missouri. In the letter, Miriam requested a copy of the marriage license "between William C. Housel and Mary Rippon in June 1888." A week later, she received copies of both the marriage application and the marriage license.

If Miriam had not by then been told the truth, she finally would have learned of her conception *before* her parents' marriage. She also learned that Mary's and Will's romance had started in Boulder, not on a ship overseas. That story was either made up by Mary to tell Miriam or made up by Miriam to tell her student Ross Ingersoll.

Armed with legal documents, Miriam traveled to Ann Arbor and signed a receipt acknowledging "Four-thousand-five-hundred dollars from James R. Housel, Roy M. Housel, and Edgar Housel as [her] share in full and [her] interest as an heir-in-law of the estate of William C. Housel, deceased." She also released and relinquished any further right, title, or interest in Will's estate which she "may have had or had." When Miriam returned to Boulder, Mary noted in her diary that Miriam brought her the deed to sign.

By then, Mary decided it was time to get the rest of her affairs in order. In January 1928, at the age of seventy-seven, she purchased a cemetery lot, in Columbia Cemetery, near the plots of her closest friends, the Bracketts and the Bells. In April 1930, she signed her "Last Will and Testament." Without stating any relationships, she wrote, "I give, devise, and bequeath all of the estate, property and effects whatsoever and wheresoever the same may be which I shall own or possess at the time of my death unto Miriam Rieder, of Boulder, Colorado, to be hers absolutely and forever."

Wilfred had entered the university as an undergraduate in the fall of 1929. Mary noted in her account book that she paid his tuition and also sent gifts of money to Anna in Germany. The two women had remained close friends. Mary lost another good friend when Auntie (Mary's aunt Hannah Skinner Hampton) died at the age of eighty-seven. Mary may have made her last trip to the bleak prairie cemetery in Fairbury, Illinois, to see her aunt buried next to her beloved uncle in January 1931.

If she traveled to her hometown of Lisbon Center, in Kendall County, she may have noticed that the ground around her father's gravestone had settled, causing the stone to begin to tilt. The two-story home built by her trust fund on her father's farm either was, or soon would be, deserted. Neighbors called it the "haunted house."

Figure 28.1 Delphine Bell (left) and Mary (right) enjoyed a mountain outing in the early 1930s.
AUTHOR'S COLLECTION

In 1934, the Boulder Fortnightly Club celebrated its fiftieth anniversary. By then, Mary was eighty-four years old. She and the club had matured together. A half century had passed since Mary had met with two friends to discuss a Ladies' Literary Club. Mary and Delphine were the only charter members still in Boulder.

Delphine's second-oldest daughter, Cleophile Bell Dean, was the club's president during its anniversary year. Mary's health had begun to decline, and she was not well enough to attend its next meeting, but Cleophile's remarks are preserved with the club's history. She stated:

> Perhaps Miss Rippon would modestly say she was just a professor, but she was more than that. One of the earliest teachers at the University, her interest in the institution never waned. For many years she gave of herself, in class and out of class, and still maintains an active interest in all that goes on, on the hill.
>
> Many have sat in Miss Rippon's classes in German, and others have enjoyed the delightful talks she gave about her numerous trips and studies abroad which, with her, were adventures in which we all shared. The new University had helped bring many to this new town and Miss Rippon, the only woman instructor, became the advisor and supervisor of the girls interested in this coeducational venture. Their problems were her problems, and she was an inspiration to all who came in contact with her. She is with us tonight in spirit although physically unable to be present.

CHAPTER 29

DURING THE LAST YEAR OF HER LIFE, MARY WROTE IN HER DIARY:

I have grown to believe that the one thing worth arriving at is simplicity of heart and life. That—

- One's relations with others should be direct and not diplomatic.
- Power leaves a bitter taste in the mouth.
- Meanness and hardness and coldness are the unforgivable sins.
- Conventionality is the mother of dreariness.
- Pleasure exists not in virtue of material conditions, but in the joyful heart.
- The world is a very interesting and beautiful place.
- Congenial labor is the secret of happiness, and many other things which seem, as I write them down, to be dull and trite commonplaces, but are for me the bright jewels which I have found beside the way.

* * *

Mary did not leave any indication that she had any regrets about how she lived her separate lives. She appeared to rise above her conflicts and see her life as a whole. She seemed to be happy and at peace.

As Mary's health again began to deteriorate, she noted that little clumps of violets bloomed by her back doorstep. In the spring of 1935, she was nearly eighty-five years old and attended by a private nurse, Mrs. A. M. Vance. Except for a few weeks when Mary was confined in bed, she got up and walked every day.

Whenever the weather cooperated, Mary took a cane and wandered in her garden. Often she sat outside in a chair. She was always neatly attired in a dress with her hair combed and pulled back in a bun. She preferred to sit with the flowers in the garden rather than cut them to bring them into the house. According to a Whitney descendant, she also loved to go out after a rain when the ground was wet and toss wildflower seeds in the wind.

Even though Mrs. Vance pressured her to rest, Mary continued to entertain friends and former students. Wilfred had graduated and was teaching art at the University of Denver, but Mary often saw Miriam as well as her nephew Norman Whitney and his family from Kansas.

One day when Mary and Norman were alone, they sat out in the garden and had a long talk. Norman and his children were Mary's only publicly known relatives. She probably took this time to explain to him that although he was identified in her will as her legal heir, she had stipulated that her entire estate was instead to go to Miriam. Mary told Norman the whole story of her separate lives, or at least most of it. She explained that she wanted Miriam to inherit her home and what little she had without publicly disclosing their mother-daughter relationship.

Norman agreed to waive his inheritance rights when the time came. According to his daughter, Joy, he did not tell his wife or the rest of his family. Mary lived on her Carnegie pension of slightly more than one hundred dollars per month, plus a quarterly stock dividend of thirty-six dollars and repayment of principal and interest on outstanding promissory notes. As always, she continued to record every household expense in her account book.

Mary's hand shook when she wrote specific instructions for her funeral. She asked that it be simple, that there be no cut flowers, and that she be buried in her plot in Columbia Cemetery near the Bracketts and the Bells. Lottie had already been interred beside J. Raymond, and one day Delphine would be buried next to her husband, James. Mary wanted her close friends and confidants in life to surround her in death as well.

In the beginning of September 1935, Mary set down her diary and account book for the last time. On the ninth of the month, she got up at six o'clock in the morning but felt immediately exhausted and fell back on her chair. Her nurse, Mrs. Vance, found her on the floor and helped her back into bed. A physician was called, but Mary died before he arrived.

A lengthy obituary was published the same day in the Boulder *Daily Camera*. It stated, in part:

> Miss Mary Rippon, 85, member of the University of Colorado faculty from the second semester of its opening year to her retirement in the summer of 1909, died this morning at 6:30 at her home, 2463 Twelfth Street . . . Death came peacefully, in keeping with the quiet life she had led since retiring from teaching—a profession that she honored." The writer mentioned that Mary never lost interest in the university or her former students and wrote, "No teacher had more friends.
>
> Miss Rippon is survived by a nephew, Norman Whitney, of Wichita [Topeka], Kansas, who recently visited her," continued the obituary. "Mrs. Miriam Rieder, assistant professor in Romance languages at the University, was one of Miss Rippon's greatest friends, and Mrs. Rieder's son, Wilfred, was her protégé.

According to her wishes, Mary's personal relationships remained secret.

Mary's funeral was held in her home. An aging crowd of mourners stepped out of their automobiles and climbed up the steps from Twelfth Street. Roses still bloomed in the garden, and their fragrance filled the air. Members of the university faculty, former students, and church friends, as well as Delphine and the ladies of the Boulder Fortnightly Club, came quietly to pay their respects.

Norman arrived in Boulder on the train. So did Tacy Mildred Brackett, daughter-in-law of the late J. Raymond and Lottie Brackett from next door. Miriam and Wilfred joined the assemblage of mourners.

According to an article in the Boulder *Daily Camera*, an a cappella choir sang songs in both German and English. Reverend Lucius F. Reed of the Congregational Church led the group in prayer and said a few words about Mary's teaching career but remembered her request to keep the service simple.

Afterward, several of the guests accompanied Mary's body to Columbia Cemetery. Surrounding homes replaced the open prairie land that Mary and Will had once known so well. Tall handsome trees shaded the casket as it was lowered into the ground.

At a later date, a small flat stone engraved with an open book and two columbines was placed on the grave. Books and flowers symbolized Mary's separate lives, both entwined on her gravestone. The books represented her teaching profession that she had shared with Joseph Sewall and her colleagues. The flowers portrayed her emotional side, her inner self that she had shared with Will. In death, the separate lives of Mary Rippon finally were combined.

In October 1935, Norman Whitney signed a "Waiver of Notice" form which stated, "I am a nephew of the said Mary Rippon, deceased, and am her sole and only heir-at-law . . . I do hereby expressly waive the service upon me of all notice which would otherwise be required of the hearing."

Figure 29.1. Mary's flat stone is engraved with an open book and two columbines symbolizing her love for learning and wildflowers.
PHOTO IN 1995 BY AUTHOR

Figure 29.2. Mary's flat gravestone (foreground) is near those of the Bell (left) and Bracket (right) families—her closest Boulder friends.
PHOTO IN 1995 BY AUTHOR

Afterward he took his daughter, Joy, to Columbia Cemetery. He explained to her why their family would not inherit Mary's property. He told her of Mary and Will's marriage and that Miriam was their daughter.

Norman also told Joy that she was never to tell her mother. In doing so, he had helped in part to preserve the secret—but he did allow the story of Mary's separate lives to move into the next generation.

PART V

MARY RIPPON REMEMBERED, 1935–PRESENT

Chapter 30

After Mary's death, alumni members met to discuss a suitable memorial. A twenty-one-member committee, including Miriam and Rosetta, was formed to start raising funds. The members sent letters all over the country requesting contributions.

One of Mary's former students, Louise Berg, of Aspen, Colorado, wrote in reply:

> I have just heard of the death of our beloved teacher and friend, Miss Mary Rippon. The sorrow I feel is too deep to express. I was one of the many whom she helped financially during college days. In the years since, we have always kept in touch with each other. And I have learned to appreciate her sweet character more and more.
>
> She was one of earth's choice spirits. Lovely and loving in thought, word, and deed. She was an inspirational teacher whose influence went far beyond the classroom.

The university had already planned improvements that included landscaping, handball courts, tennis courts, an addition to the theater building, and an outdoor theater. President George Norlin requested that the outdoor theater become Mary's memorial. The regents voted their approval and stated that an appropriation, not to exceed seven hundred fifty dollars, would be paid from their general fund. The university received additional funds for the theater and the other projects from the federal Works Progress Administration.

Headlines in the *Denver Post* read, "C. U. Plans Big Outdoor Theater as Memorial to Mary Rippon." The article stated that the twelve-hundred-seat structure would be immediately south of the

Hellems liberal arts building. Once the building's wings were added, the theater would be inside a protected court. By February 1936, some of the trees had been moved in preparation for the theater's construction.

At the time, the country was suffering through the Great Depression, but many of Mary's former friends were quick to respond to the fund-raising request. Checks for one, two, or five dollars were accompanied with apologies by those unable to send any more. A few contributors wrote checks for one hundred dollars. With every check came a letter.

Jessie Stanton Dakan, of Longmont, Colorado, wrote:

> We attended her classes in Old Main some forty years ago, and no memorial built by human hands can equal the ones built in the hearts of 'her boys and girls' by her daily contact with them through the years. Her kindly smile, her sympathetic understanding, and her desire to help made her life one lived for others. May the memorial be symbolic of that spirit.

Another former student asked:

> Do the lilies of the valley still grow everywhere in her garden? I remember she had brought the pips from Germany, and they became naturalized in her lovely garden. Perhaps, someday, some of them could be moved to the campus in the vicinity of the theater. She loved them, and they are modest and lovely as she was.

"Alumni day" was held on June 13, 1936. Although the Mary Rippon Theater, as it was called, was only partially completed at the time, the committee still held its dedication. Men in suits and women in summery dresses with hats and gloves sat under the shade of the remaining trees. The speakers faced them from an improvised lectern under another tree.

Students in the Germanic languages department sang Mary's favorite song, *Ach, wie ist's moglich dann*, which translates into English as "How can I leave thee?" President Norlin explained that the dedication was being held that day at the request of many of her former pupils. Then came their comments.

Figure 30.1. "Mary Rippon Theater" is still visible on the wall in front of the outdoor theater on the university campus.
PHOTO BY AUTHOR, 1995

Dr. Timothy Stanton, the paleontologist from the class of 1883, reminisced about the university's early days and said, "Miss Rippon's name brought to mind all that is noblest and best in womanhood."

He continued:

> In every kind of problem that came up in a student's life, whether the difficulty was due to financial straits, or lack of mental discipline, or spiritual confusion, if the person was honest and straightforward in his endeavor to do the right thing, Miss Rippon's sympathetic aid was always quickly available. Any student of the early days can give you numerous examples of her generous help along these lines either from his own experience or from the testimony of his associates—but never from anything Miss Rippon said.
>
> . . . I could speak from personal experience myself, but the details of such memories are too sacred to be held up to public gaze. Her little

cottage on Twelfth Street was for many years a shrine which I never failed to visit when that was possible.

Dr. Amy Miles, a member of the class of 1902, praised the work that had been done in starting the memorial and the quick response of the alumni. She said, "How like her the columbine, God's perfect flower."

Faculty member and former student Edna Davis Romig wrote a "Poem for Miss Rippon," that read:

> The quiet of her flowers was on her life,
> But it was quiet of no shallow plant
> Blooming a colored day to fade at night;
> Hers was the bloom of all slow-growing things
> Deep in the subsoil rooted, knowing strife,
> Knowing the forces that can twist and slant,
> The heat that shrivels and the winds that blight.
>
> Hers was the quiet of strong folded wings
> After the valorous flight. Hers was the peace
> Of the great adventure. Hers the high passage
> And safe return . . . A pioneer she came
> Unfearing; unafraid she lived and taught
> Youth the adventure of the mind's release.
>
> A gentle woman with a brave message,
> A kindly counsel, and a torch, a flame
> Illuminating corridors of thought.
> She built of substances transcending time:
> We build in stone but trust to honor more
> The spirit of her building—in the shadow
> Of hills she loved, erect these stones, restore
> Her old devotion now to Colorado
> And give her timeless, to a future time.
>
> Dear friend and teacher, can you hear our words—
> You of the silvered hair and fine blue eyes

You in the sprigged challis dress, blue as the eyes
That looked straight into ours in kindliness
And counsel? We would learn your quiet way
With beauty and the old simplicities
Of life—your garden peace when violets
Flowered quietly and columbines
At twilight floated like a phantom troop
Of moths and butterflies, where every flower
Gave perfume, and Madonna lilies bloomed
For your delight. Do you know now, dear friend,
Our gratitude for all you taught of life
And living, and the deep contentment of
Good books; of drama, poetry, and works
Grown golden through the wisdom of the years?

We speak but simply, and our weak words fall
Far short of uttering that inner truth
That you were able to communicate.
Yet we remember all—your flowers, your books,
Your total message, your beloved Yourself.
Young feet have still their journey—may they go
Sometimes in paths made gracious by your going.

May young eyes see at times the golden morning.
The azure dusk you saw. May young minds know
Today, tomorrow, what yesterday you knew:
The living drama we are actors in
And what the part we play not wholly is
Determined by the cue of Destiny.

If Mary could have heard her friends that day, she might have been moved by their sentiments and graciously accepted their recognition. Perhaps, though, they would have been surprised if they knew that the woman they all admired had once written "conventionality is the mother of dreariness."

CHAPTER 31

IN THE SPRING OF 1935, THE ROMANCE LANGUAGE FACULTY HELD A "steak fry" for all of the promising students in the department. By then, Miriam had been promoted from instructor to assistant professor. Ross Ingersoll and another of Miriam's students were asked to do the work of supplying and preparing the food. Since neither of the students had a car, Miriam volunteered to drive them around town in Mary's aging Chevrolet as they looked for the best food they could find within a given budget.

Then, on the day of the event, she again drove them to the various stores to pick up the food and transport it to the Flagstaff Mountain picnic area. Having become acquainted with Miriam during the preparations for this event, Ross took to dropping by Miriam's second-floor office in Old Main for a chat and a cigarette between classes.

In corresponding with the author in 1997, for the first edition of this book, the late Dr. Ross Ingersoll wrote:

> Miriam's participation at the picnic had been unusual, but since she was a member of the faculty, she was more or less obliged to attend. She didn't like parties to begin with and objected to this one in particular, as she considered it to be a very obvious ruse for recruiting new majors. She had very few personal friends on the faculty and wasn't often involved in their social affairs. Her son Wilfred had graduated the year before, and she was lonely and needed someone with whom to talk.

Throughout the next few years, Miriam and her student became very good friends. She told him a great deal about herself and a little about Mary. Miriam invited very few people to her home, and Ross was pleased and flattered to have been one of those who got to listen to her enormous collection of records, have a few drinks, and talk.

Ingersoll recalled an afternoon in 1936 when he and Miriam were relaxing after class and each sipping a Tom Collins in her living room. Unexpectedly, Miriam said that she wanted to tell him something but asked him to promise never to tell anyone unless the occasion demanded it. She then revealed that Mary was her mother. Miriam assured him that, at that time, even Wilfred did not know.

Ingersoll added, "Whenever Miriam spoke of Mary, she always referred to her as 'my aunt' or 'Aunt Mary.'"

Miriam told her friend the romanticized version that either Mary had told her, or that Miriam had made up to save the embarrassment of revealing the whole truth. Miriam said she wanted someone to know that Mary was her mother, as she was afraid that if she suddenly died, her former husband, Rudolf Rieder, might come to Boulder and try to claim her property. In their conversation she called Rudolf "cruel and unfeeling." (Miriam and Rudolf had divorced in 1922, but her students continued to call her "Mrs. Rieder.")

After Miriam inherited Mary's house, she rented it out for a few months. Then Rudolf's brother and wife came to Boulder and needed a place to stay. Perhaps in an effort to keep peace within the family, Miriam kicked out her tenants and let her former in-laws live there for the winter. Dr. Ingersoll remembers being invited over for "genuine German pancakes." A year or two later, the cottage was sold.

Like Mary, Miriam preferred wildflowers to cultivated formal gardens. She and Ross often drove to an open field on North Broadway to search for the first anemones of early spring. According to Dr. Ingersoll, Miriam had very definite feelings about whom she liked and did not like. She was often outspoken, angry, and bitter. She could be very gracious, but it was easy to get on her blacklist and, once on, almost impossible to get off. As Ingersoll later recalled, "She could be really nasty to people she did not like or to those whom she thought had taken advantage of her."

Miriam's home on South Broadway had been convenient to campus, but, in Dr. Ingersoll's opinion, Miriam resented her neighbors just for being close. She coveted her privacy and moved to a one-story brick bungalow with several undeveloped acres south of the Boulder city limits. She lived with several dogs of varying breed, size, and color and never remarried. In the winter, when she depended upon wood for added warmth, she would haul a ten- or fifteen-foot branch or log to the fireplace and prop the log on chairs to feed into the fire as needed.

The brick house at 1604 Bluebell Avenue still stands, and a blue spruce grows in front. Along the west side are planted cottonwoods, maples, and a linden tree. South and east of the house are an apricot tree, wild plums, and chokecherries.

As Boulder inched outward, Miriam preserved as much as she could of the wild and unkempt prairie. Additional native plants and flowers provided a sanctuary for ground-nesting birds. Not everyone appreciated her efforts. After a neighbor complained of allergies from her "weeds,"

Figure 31.1. For much of Miriam's teaching career, she and her dogs lived in this bungalow at 1604 Bluebell Avenue, now within Boulder's city limits.
CARNEGIE LIBRARY FOR LOCAL HISTORY, BOULDER

Miriam defended her property with a scathing letter to the editor of the Boulder *Daily Camera*. In it, she asked:

> How can people go to church and sit in pews and worship God, and then devote their weekdays to trying to destroy what He has generously given us to enjoy?
>
> What in the name of Heaven is the matter with people who are so blind that they can see beauty, and utility, only in their own little clipped lawn, and gardens with plants of their choosing in neat, tiresome rows? All the richness and glorious beauty of the autumn landscape, with its diapason of color—gold, umbers, burnt sienna and scarlets, is lost on them. They froth at the mouth at the sight or mention of the lovely mullein, called 'Candlesticks of the Little Lord Jesus' in the gracious country where I did part of my growing up. The delicate and graceful wild lettuce with little, joyous finches swinging on its branches, is just a 'weed' to them.

Miriam regularly patrolled her property and carried a firearm, likely a shotgun, to scare off intruders. A "feud" developed after parents of neighboring children complained that Miriam chased and shot at them. In 1950, she pleaded innocent in court to "disturbing the peace" and "threatening the lives of young people." Miriam admitted to firing her gun, but said she aimed at a clay bank and did it only to frighten the children from her property. She had told her university classes that she planned to bequeath her property to the city of Boulder, but she withdrew the offer after the incident.

Nancy Atkins Ferriss, a student of Italian in the 1950s, said that in her generation at the university, teachers were expected to fit into a mold, but Miriam never did. "Her appearance was of absolutely no importance," Ferriss said. "She would have been perfectly at home in the 1960s or 1970s, but she was out of place in the 1950s." Some of her other students referred to her as "Bohemian."

According to Ferriss, Miriam was very much her own person. Clothing was meant to be warm and comfortable. If her slip showed or colors did not match, it made no difference to her. A tam was her only hat. Long

Figure 31.2. Miriam curled her hair for this portrait in May 1950.
Charles F. Snow photographs, COU:1483, Box 160, Item 38768, Rare and
Distinctive Collections, University of Colorado Boulder Libraries

ago, she had regained her lost weight and again was slightly plump. Her hair was chopped off, severely straight, and not styled.

Although uninterested in her own clothing, Miriam had comments on the clothing of others. She wrote another letter to the editor of the newspaper in favor of female students wearing blue jeans and untucked shirts to class. She began by writing:

> You asked for this, in fact you begged for it, so here goes! It is none of your business what the coeds wear. Speaking as one who knows coeds, I should like to say that the girls who come here to work and who are not always thinking about their looks, are the ones worth the taxpayers' money. You can have the primping cuties who live with a mirror in one hand and a lipstick in the other . . . You probably want a female according to the current dopey ditty who 'purrs like a kitten and is pink and white as a nursery.' Did you ever hear that purring kittens frequently grow up to be snarling cats, and that pink and white is no longer so nifty at fifty?

Miriam went on to describe the practicality of blue jeans in cold weather and the laundry headaches of frilly clothing. She ended her letter by saying, "There is no law against jeans and floating shirts. I like what is inside of them much better than I like clotheshorses and dressmakers' dummies."

Another student, Rosalie DeBacker Alldredge, remembered the great interest Miriam took in her students. Alldredge mentioned that a boy she was dating had decided not to come back to the university for the second semester. Miriam would not allow that to happen. "She came and got me," Alldredge said, "and we drove to his home in the southern part of the state. Between the two of us, we convinced him to return to school. He packed his things and drove back with us in her car."

"That year he took me to the junior prom," Alldredge continued. "Before we went, she [Mrs. Rieder] wanted us to come by to show her our evening clothes for the prom. When we did, she found fault with the color of my hose and lent me a pair of hers. Could I ever forget a teacher who cared for me like that?"

Miriam told her students about meeting Rudolf Rieder when he was her German literature professor in college, crossing into Italy during World War I, and of Rudolf's desire to join up with Adolf Hitler. Miriam also acknowledged that both her marriage and that of her parents had been unhappy. One year during a final exam, Miriam broke into tears and spoke about the cruelty and stubbornness of the Germans. The incident had been prompted by the suicide of one of her students whose strict and dogmatic father would not let him choose his own profession.

With Ross Ingersoll, Miriam often talked about her father. She always spoke of Will as a brilliant scholar, but she made no mention of what he had done—or not done—to earn a living.

Like Mary, Miriam took time from her teaching to travel and study in Europe. Although she was not outwardly religious, Miriam's interest in birds brought her to a study of St. Francis, which in turn took her to Assisi, Italy. In 1953, she filled out a form for the university's news bureau and listed her hobbies as "dogs, birds, squirrels, etc. etc." Occasionally she brought one or more of her dogs to class.

Her classes, like Mary's, were held in Old Main. When the weather was good, Miriam opened a window during class, made a clicking sound, and fed peanuts to squirrels on the windowsill. Most of the students in her class either studied music or were Italian-Americans interested in learning their parents' native language. The students were convinced the squirrels understood Italian. Will's ivy still grew on the side of the building below the window.

Susan Huck Carpenter was one of a small Italian class of twelve or thirteen who gathered in a local restaurant called the Sink. There, Miriam assembled her students around a big table where they all drank coffee and ate dessert. Then Miriam passed out the words to "*O Sole Mio*" and other Italian songs, and the class would sing together in Italian.

In correspondence with the author, Carpenter stated, "Everyone else in the restaurant thought we were crazy, but I adored this woman and thank her often for imparting her love of learning."

Miriam also kept up her interest in Italian opera, the topic of her master's thesis, by driving with friend Hortense Brant to see *Pasquale* and other operas performed in the opera house in the mountain town of Central City.

Until very near the end of her life, Miriam continued to keep the circumstances of her birth a secret. In 1955, she applied for a Social Security number. In the space for father's name, she wrote "William Cephas Housel," but under mother's name she wrote "Unknown."

Ross Ingersoll knew the truth, but he, too, kept the secret. So did Joy Whitney, who had married and become Joy Whitney Ahlborn. Miriam's half-brothers kept the knowledge of Mary and Will's marriage within the Housel family. Delphine Bell died in 1945 and was buried next to her husband. Rosetta Bell Wolcott may have told the secret to her daughter, Evelyn, and William Brackett may have heard the story from his parents, but it is unlikely that any of these people told anyone else.

In 1956, Miriam retired. By then, she had sold off some of her property, but only to people who agreed not to cut down the trees. She transferred her house and remaining property to herself and Wilfred in joint tenancy. Inside her home, occasional visitors had to make a path on the hardwood floors to get through piles of books and stacks of papers and magazines. Outside everything was overgrown, just as Miriam liked it.

She may never have accepted the fact that Mary was her mother. According to Dr. Ingersoll, "Never, never, even after she told me the secret, did she ever refer to Mary as her mother."

At some point, Miriam did confide in Wilfred, but publicly she—like Mary—took the secret to her grave. At the age of sixty-eight, and in her own home, Miriam died of cancer on September 26, 1957.

Wilfred may have seen what Miriam had written on her application for a Social Security number, or else he took it upon himself (at the time) to perpetuate the secret of Mary's separate lives. As the informant on Miriam's death certificate, in the space for her mother's name, he, too, simply wrote "Unknown."

Nearly two decades would pass before Wilfred donated Mary's diaries and account books to the university archives. By then, Wilfred knew that Mary's story needed to be told.

CHAPTER 32

In October 2000, former Boulder *Daily Camera* writer Clint Talbott wrote a newspaper column titled, "No sheepskin for CU trailblazer." Talbott's article reflected on this author's unsuccessful application, in 1998, to nominate Mary for a doctor of humane letters honorary degree from the University of Colorado. Although several prominent university figures strongly supported the nomination, the university regents turned it down—even though they freely granted honorary posthumous *bachelor's* degrees. No explanation for the rejected Rippon nomination was given, but, with a little prodding, it became evident that the regents' policy on honorary *doctoral* degrees was that they were reserved for the living.

Talbott quoted then-Boulder City Councilman Dan Corson, also a historian, who reiterated that Mary did as much or more than any professor or president to build the university's reputation. Corson then stated, "She is unique in the University of Colorado's history, and the powers that be at CU shouldn't be concerned that other similarly qualified applicants will pop up out of the woodwork."

"Darn right," quipped Talbott. "Sensible leaders know that rules are rules, but good judgment is a matter of degree." His comment must have resonated, as a few years later "the powers that be" had a change of heart. In November 2005, after professor and chair of the Department of Sociology Michael L. Radelet started a new nomination for Mary to get an honorary degree, it was approved. regent and chair of the Honorary Degree Committee Cindy Carlisle stated, "Rippon shattered the glass ceilings of the day. Not only was she a scholar and a teacher; she was a revolutionary. She was a magnet for students who were ready to break the mold."

* * *

Professor Radelet, in his cover letter to the Board of Regents, provided information that the regents may not have known in 1998, specifically that Mary had never received any college degree at all, not even a bachelor's. "Her record in building this university is second to none," stated Radelet, "and, as such, it is entirely appropriate for CU to award her its highest honor." He also mentioned the 1999 publication of this book, and that the prior attempt to award Mary a degree had been unsuccessful.

Radelet then explained that in the few short years between the nominations, the university had redoubled its efforts to expand its diversity and make the campus more attentive to gender issues. "Honoring Professor [Mary] Rippon's achievements is one small step that helps create a more gender-inclusive environment," wrote Radelet. "In short, awarding this honorary degree is good for all of us." He added that scores of top leaders on the Boulder campus had enthusiastically added their endorsements, and all showed overwhelming support for Mary's proposed honorary degree.

Many of the letters simply voiced their approval, but other letters and emails included comments. History professor Lee Chambers touched on Mary's separate lives when she wrote, "She is a fascinating case of gender discrimination, gender difference, and sexual outlawry in American society and academe! I support this effort strongly."

Adding to the many individual endorsements was the unanimous support of whole departments, including deans, department chairs, and program directors. The most vocal supporters came from the departments of sociology, history, theatre/dance, and Germanic/Slavic languages and literatures. Still more came from the women's studies program and the women's studies resource center, followed by the interim chancellor and the university's president, Hank Brown. Added to that list were all of the members of the still-existing Boulder Fortnightly Club, director Kay Oltmans of the University of Colorado Heritage Center, and Martie

McMane, senior minister of Boulder's First Congregational Church that Mary had attended.

The nomination form required three letters of support. Letters for both the 1998 and the 2005 nominations were submitted from Adrian Del Caro (PhD, professor of German studies, comparative literature and humanities, and who also served as undergraduate associate chair, Germanic and Slavic languages and literatures) and Albert Allen Bartlett (PhD, professor emeritus, Department of Physics).

Dr. Del Caro, who today is a distinguished professor at University of Tennessee-Knoxville, reviewed the life and times in which Mary lived while also outlining her many accomplishments. In addition, both in the 1998 and 2005 applications, he wrote:

> This matter is of personal and professional interest to me because since joining the faculty here at CU in 1992, I have served in two positions formerly held by Professor Rippon. For seven years I chaired Germanic and Slavic Languages and Literatures, and I am also a professor of German who happens to teach, among other things, Goethe's *Faust*—which Mary Rippon first taught during her tenure at CU during the 1870s. More recently I served as associate vice chancellor for graduate education and associate dean of the Graduate School, in this capacity developing a deeper sense of our institution's responsibility for the delivery of graduate education, in particular for preparing doctoral candidates.

In conclusion, Dr. Del Caro wrote that Mary's lack of a degree was a "gap of nearly tragic proportions that this woman held no academic credentials, despite the fact that she proved herself again and again under the most trying circumstances." He then added, "I am concerned that our university will be upstaged, quite frankly, by another institution, and Colorado will not be the first to honor its cherished professor. In short, the award of an honorary PhD to Professor Mary Rippon has my very strongest support."

Dr. Albert Bartlett, one of the most renowned professors at the university, gave additional background on Mary's teaching career, adding that she also served as the unofficial Dean of Women for many years.

In his reflection on her life and achievements, for both nominations he stated:

> It is always proper that the University examine its early history and give fitting recognition, often long overdue, to the pioneer educators who struggled to bring culture and scholarship to the young students of the remote western frontier. They were laboring in one of the first institutions of higher education in a vast expanse of western America. Mary Rippon stands out as one of the great members of the hardy band of educators who set the stage for the great University of Colorado that we enjoy today.
>
> By awarding Mary Rippon an honorary doctorate, *honoris causa*, the University will be recognizing her outstanding and pioneering contributions to the educational mission of the University. This is an opportunity for the University to express its thanks and appreciation to Mary Rippon for her long life of teaching and service to the University, to Boulder, and to the people of Colorado.

The first nomination also included letters from the Heritage Center's director Kay Oltmans, as well as W. E. Briggs, professor emeritus of mathematics and former dean of the College of Arts and Sciences. Wendy Hall, branch manager of Boulder's Carnegie Branch Library for Local History, contributed a letter for the second nomination, emphasizing Mary's legacy in the community and her contributions to "town and gown."

After the second nomination, the regents' Honorary Degree Committee announced the names of its awardees—including Mary—at its March 2, 2006, meeting. Wilfred had died in 1986, but Professor Radelet wasted no time contacting Wilfred's son (Mary's great-grandson), Eric Rieder. Mary's professional accomplishments finally would be publicly recognized, and Rieder's presence would bring her separate lives into the twenty-first century. Rieder immediately made plans to attend spring commencement in Boulder's Folsom Field in May 2006.

CHAPTER 33

FRIDAY, MAY 12, 2006, DAWNED SUNNY AND WARM. THE GATES TO FOLsom Field, the university's stadium, opened at 7 a.m., with commencement starting at 8:30 a.m. The scene was joyous and the music loud as friends and family seated themselves in the bleachers while the graduates took their seats on the field. Before the ceremony was over, the university granted a total of 5,610 degrees, but only a few recipients, including Eric Rieder, were invited onto the podium. As the jumbotron flashed the scene to an estimated twenty thousand spectators, Todd Gleeson, dean of the College of Arts and Sciences, spoke a few words and Chancellor Philip P. DiStefano presented Rieder with Mary's diploma.

The diploma read:

The Regents of the
University of Colorado
have conferred on
Mary Rippon
the Honorary Degree
Doctor of Humane Letters
Honoris Causa
with all the rights and privileges thereunto appertaining.
In witness thereof this diploma is awarded by the Regents
Signed and Sealed on the twelfth day of May, A.D.
two thousand and six in the
one hundred thirtieth year of the University.

Paul D. Schauer   Hank Brown
Chair, Board of Regents   President of the University

Millie Cortez   Philip P. DiStefano
Secretary   Chancellor

In recent email correspondence with the author, Rieder reflected on the notification of Mary's honorary degree and his travel to Boulder to accept the diploma. "To say I was surprised is an understatement," he stated. "It was like the opening up of a time capsule on the past. The hospitality and warmth afforded me and my family was wonderful, and I will never forget the honor and privilege it was to accept Mary's degree at graduation. I'm sure Mary, Miriam, and my Dad were thrilled that this honor and recognition was bestowed on Mary."

* * *

Mary's honorary degree transcended the past by bringing her distinguished place in history into the present day. But it wasn't the only posthumous recognition she would receive. Julia Frey (now Julia Nolet), a professor of French at the university from 1976 to 2001, had learned of and was impressed with Mary's story. On August 31, 2020—fourteen years after Eric Rieder's acceptance of Mary's honorary degree—Nolet established the "Mary Rippon Endowed Scholarship Fund for Single Parents."

In Nolet's "Statement of Donor Intent," she specified that the scholarship funds were to be used to provide awards for in-state students enrolled at the University of Colorado, in Boulder. Qualified student applicants would be single parents and/or those providing the sole support for their child/children. Nolet added that women were particularly encouraged to apply, but an applicant's gender would not be considered a factor in the recipient selection process.

At the time of this writing, two young women have received the Mary Rippon Scholarship: the first during the 2020–2021 academic year and the second in 2021–2022. Both are raising sons, and both have bright futures. The first recipient graduated with a major in mechanical engineering. The young woman wrote to Nolet that the money allowed her to be able to stay focused on school and to spend more quality time with her son. The second recipient, a computer science major, juggled both school and her son's care with a paying job. She used her scholarship funds for her internet connection, lunches, and books she needed for her classes.

Figure 33.1. Eric Rieder, great-grandson of Mary Rippon, accepted her honorary doctoral degree from chancellor Philip P. DiStefano.
CASEY A. CASS, UNIVERSITY OF COLORADO

In recent correspondence with the author, Nolet credited the first edition of *Separate Lives* with bringing Mary out of the shadows. But Mary's biography is only part of her story. Ever since 1936, the university has kept her name alive in the Mary Rippon Theater. Then, quietly and throughout the decades, Mary's grandson, Wilfred, carefully preserved her diaries and account books before donating them to the University of Colorado Archives. Wilfred also spent the final five years of his life recording his own (unpublished) memories of Mary.

In 1985, Mary was posthumously honored by a volunteer non-profit—the Colorado Women's Hall of Fame. According to the organization's website, its inductees are chosen from "women who were not only accomplished in their professions and/or the community" but "women who also raised the bar, set a new standard, opened or widened the opportunities for others, and through their positive accomplishments led the way for future generations."

Figure 33.2. After the ceremony, professor Mike Radelet, Eric Rieder, and the author (Silvia Pettem) posed with Mary's diploma.
AUTHOR'S COLLECTION

Mary did all that and was a mother too.

The twenty-first century has added even more chapters to Mary's legacy. At Boulder's Columbia Cemetery, her grave is featured on history tours that bring to mind Will's long-ago sentiments that "a spirit sometimes lingers in a blossom or a tree." Her new accolades, along with her posthumous honorary degree, followed by the Mary Rippon Scholarship have guaranteed Mary's place in the university for years to come. Nolet called the scholarship "one of the continuing ripples in Mary's life story." No doubt there will be many more.

Acknowledgments

I am grateful to many people who contributed to my research and helped me with this project, both for the first edition published in 1999 and this recent edition in 2024. Of most importance in the first edition were Edgar Searles Housel and Robert P. Housel, both grandsons of William C. Housel, and Barbara Parrish, who told me where to find them. Jerry Winters Housel, nephew of William C. "Will" Housel, and Joy Whitney Ahlborn, great-niece of Mary Rippon, also contributed valuable primary source material.

Additional family history came from Roland Wolcott, grandson of Louisa Bixby Wolcott, second wife of Will's father, Peter Housel. Roland's sister, Evelyn Wolcott; wife, Jewel Wolcott; and daughter, Rachel Wolcott, also aided me in uncovering photos and documents that helped to more fully document Mary Rippon's and Will Housel's lives. In addition, the Wolcott family supplied me with information on the Bell family, from whom they are descended.

In 1998, I traveled to Kendall County, Illinois, and was fortunate to meet Thomas Fletcher Sr. and Thomas Fletcher Jr., who showed me their properties, as well as Orville and Ardella Orton, who provided information on the Lisbon Cemetery. I was also grateful to Ardys B. Hughes and Tricia Inman, who supplied me with Mary's guardianship records from the Kendall County Circuit Court, and to Charlene Austin, Goldie Behrens, and Carol Fowler, who helped me with property records at the Kendall County Recorder's Office in Yorkville, Illinois. Thanks, too, to Ruth Fletcher Bell and Marvin Lawyer for additional information on Kendall County.

At the University of Colorado Boulder, I was very thankful for the assistance of Dr. Adrian Del Caro, professor of German and chair of the Department of Germanic and Slavic Languages and Literatures, for his expertise in the interpretation of Goethe's *Faust*. Lee Chambers-Schiller, associate professor in the History Department, advised me on incorporating historic context; Julia Frey (now Julia Nolet), associate professor in the French and Italian Departments, aided me in a French translation; and both director of the University of Colorado Heritage Center Kay Oltmans and the late professor emeritus (Department of Physics) Albert Allen Bartlett went out of their way to aid me in my research.

Longtime friends and colleagues also shared their enthusiasm and expertise. Lois Anderton was the first to bring the story of Mary Rippon to my attention. Others who contributed to my research included Marti Anderson (who advised me to put my "gut feelings" into words), William Arndt, Jeanne Baur, Jody Corruccini, Marty Covey, Wendy Hall, David Hays, Laurence Paddock, and Cassandra Volpe. I also wish to thank Robb Abramson, Karl Anuta, Jane Barker, Maxine Benson, Jody Berman, Anne Dyni, Scott Havlick, Diana Korte, Tom Meier, Bruce Montgomery, Tom Noel, Fred Pruett, Mary Jo Reitsema, MaryKay Scott, Boyce Sher, Charlotte Smokler, Mary Brackett Vandagriff, Elliott West, and the student assistants at the Archives Department in the University of Colorado's Norlin Library.

Many others responded to my requests for personal information on Mary Rippon and Miriam Rieder. I wish to thank Rosalie DeBacker Alldredge, Mitzi Baier, Peter Bessol, Hortense Brant, Christopher and Margot Brauchli, Susan Huck Carpenter, Anna Goodykoontz Edmonds, Nancy Atkins Ferriss, Francis J. Geck, Barbara A. Hodge, Richard E. King, Ruby Marr, Henry Cord Meyer, John Munro, Alberta Nicholson, E. Thomas Punshon, Marilyn Reed, Margaret B. Stockman, Louise Wicks, and especially Dr. Ross Ingersoll.

Archivists and librarians around the country provided me with their own primary source materials, as well. The bulk of my research for the first edition was done the old-fashioned way, with letters and telephone calls. I would like to thank the following correspondents in their former positions: David J. Brough (secretary of the Genealogical Society of Washtenaw County in Ann Arbor, Michigan), Deb Duhr (librarian at Fulton Public Library in Fulton, Illinois), Kathy Flynn (collections manager of the Peabody Essex Museum in Salem, Massachusetts), Verda Gerwick (president of the Lexington Genealogical and Historical Society, Inc. in Lexington, Illinois), Patricia A. Hamilton (director of the Pontiac Public Library, Pontiac, Illinois), Margie Hedrick (librarian at the Dominy Memorial Library in Fairbury, Illinois), and Karen L. Jania (reference assistant at Bentley Historical Library, University of Michigan).

I also wish to thank the following, also in their former positions: Thomas M. Kirk (archivist at University of Wisconsin-Madison Archives), Hope Lynch (archivist at the Delta Gamma Executive Office, Columbus, Ohio), Becca Marinelli (archivist at the Catholic Charities and Community Services, Lakewood, Colorado), Halyne Myroniuk (assistant curator at the Immigration History Research Center, St. Paul, Minnesota), Roger Platt (intern archivist at Illinois State University, Normal, Illinois), John Y. Simon (executive director the Ulysses S. Grant Association, in Carbondale, Illinois), Deborah Steffes (librarian at Morris Area Public Library, Morris, Illinois), Carol L. Sykes (deputy register of Washtenaw County, Ann Arbor, Michigan), Warren E. Taylor (special collections librarian at Topeka and Shawnee County Public Library, Topeka, Kansas), and Sandy Tracy (Fulton County Historical and Genealogical Society, Canton, Illinois).

Special thanks go to the first edition's editor, Elaine Long, who helped me more than she knows. I am also grateful for the support of my late father, Franz Veith, and his wife, Nelly Veith, who helped with translations of French and German correspondence.

In preparation for the 2024 edition, I appreciated the conscientious editing by Brittany Stoner at Lyons Press, as well as thoughts shared and correspondence with fellow author and foreword writer Julia Bricklin. For content, I am especially thankful to Michael L. Radelet (professor emeritus, Department of Sociology). Not only was he the driving force for Mary Rippon's posthumous honorary degree in 2006, he preserved his correspondence files and, nearly two decades later, enthusiastically and graciously shared them with me. I also am extremely grateful for my correspondence with Mary's great-grandson, Eric Rieder, and his wife Phyllis Rieder.

Additional friends and colleagues in the Boulder and the university communities also became part of Mary Rippon's story in their association with her honorary degree and scholarship. In addition to Dr. Adrian Del Caro, Michael L. Radelet, and Eric and Phyllis Rieder are the following, listed with brief descriptions at the time of Mary's degree in 2006:

- Albert Allen Bartlett (professor emeritus, Department of Physics)
- W. E. Briggs (professor emeritus, Mathematics, and former dean of the College of Arts and Sciences)
- Hank Brown (president, University of Colorado)
- Cindy Carlisle (regent and chair of the Honorary Degree Committee)
- Casey A. Cass (University of Colorado photographer)
- Lee Chambers (professor of history)
- Dan Corson (Boulder city councilman)
- Philip P. DiStefano (University of Colorado chancellor)
- Julia Frey, now Julia Nolet (professor emeritus of French)
- Wendy Hall (Branch manager, Boulder's Carnegie Branch Library for Local History)
- Martie McMane (senior minister, Boulder's First Congregational Church)
- Kay Oltmans, (director, University of Colorado Heritage Center)
- Clint Talbott (Boulder *Daily Camera* writer)

Appendix: Mary Rippon's and Will Housel's Diaries

January 6, 1892–June 23, 1892

January 6, Rippon: "W. [Will]."

January 6, Housel: "Husked corn."

January 7, Rippon: "School, Fortnightly and faculty meeting left me tired."
January 7, Housel: "Baled hay."

January 8, Rippon: "4 recitations, 1 period in chapel. Faculty meeting 4–7."
January 8, Housel: "Baled hay."

January 9, Rippon: "Mrs. Linder came. Swept and cleaned. Letter from Mrs. [Lizzie] Ellet. One from Helen and Mamie with photo. Went to Mr. [Sidney A.] Giffin's. Called on Mrs. Whitney and Mrs. Grovesnor."
January 9, Housel: "Baled hay till noon."

Sunday January 10, Rippon: "Church and charity. Cold, below zero. Went to see Mrs. Greene. W. [Will] came."
Sunday January 10, Housel: "Went to B. [Boulder] PM. Came home in snow and cold wave. M. [Mary]."

January 11, Rippon: "Below zero. Wrote Vira and Mr. Campbell."
January 11, Housel: "Cold. Worked 40# of butter and a new churning."

January 12, Rippon: "Miss [Caroline M.] Hyde called. Will came a moment."
January 12, Housel: "Cold. Went to town PM."

January 13, Rippon: "Hung pictures in Fortnightly room. Water pipes burst, horrible."
January 13, Housel: "Took Ed [Edgar Housel] to Louisville. Let him have $10. Jim and Charlie went to Davidson's for the pig. Cold. M. [Mary]."

January 14, Rippon: "Did not attend faculty meeting nor Fortnightly."
January 14, Housel: "Husked corn till noon. Put up ice PM."

January 15, Rippon: "Cold. W. [Will] came. Took French class."
January 15, Housel: "Put up ice. Went to B. [Boulder]. M. [Mary]."

January 16, Rippon: "Very cold. Attended Delta Gamma at Mandi's. Called on Mrs. Cullen. Slept at Mrs. [Elizabeth] Mallon's. Mrs. [Delphine] Bell called."
January 16, Housel: "Finished the corn. Cold wave coming."

Sunday January 17, Rippon: "Church and charity. Miriam's birthday. Will came to dinner."
Sunday January 17, Housel: "Went to church. Stayed up till evening. Snowing. M. [Mary]."

January 18, Rippon: "New semester. Very cold. Called on Mrs. Giffin. Mrs. [Ida] Rosenkrans called."
January 18, Housel: "Cold. Hired man left. Talked with father about the farm. Agreed."

January 19, Rippon: "Sudden change to warm weather. Telegram from Mrs. [Lizzie] Ellet. Letter from Vira."
January 19, Housel: "Took load of hay to Rutter. Fixed fence at stacks."

January 20, Rippon: "Mrs. [Lizzie] Ellet came. Faculty meeting. Wrote Holt my thanks for Whitney's Fr. [French] Reader.
January 20, Housel: "Put corn in loft. Mended halters and barn. Worked butter PM."

January 21, Rippon: "Calls from [visits by] Mrs. [Sarah] North and Stoddard. Mrs. [Elizabeth] Mallon left for Kansas City."

January 22, Rippon: "Prepared for Sunday. Saw the Bells."
January 22, Housel: "Killed pigs."

January 23, Rippon: "61 [photographic] negatives. Very tired."
January 23, Housel: "Took pigs to town. Got quarter of beef. Cut down trees."

Sunday January 24, Rippon: "Sermon on church and charity. W. [Will] came."
Sunday January 24, Housel: "Went to B. [Boulder] PM. M. [Mary]."

January 25, Rippon: "Fred Unfug's funeral. Went to the [Sidney A.] Giffins'."
January 25, Housel: "Made sausage."

January 26, Rippon: "Returned 2 books to Dr. [J. Raymond] Brackett."
January 26, Housel: "Baled hay."

January 27, Rippon: "Made several slides. Called to see Mrs. [Lottie] Brackett. Mrs. [Delphine] Bell went with me."
January 27, Housel: "Baled hay."

January 28, Rippon: "Fortnightly."
January 28, Housel: "Baled hay."

January 29, Rippon: "Reception at Dr. [J. Raymond] Brackett's."
January 29, Housel: "Went to Farmers Institute in Longmont. Hotel $2.00, Stable $0.50, Dinner $0.25."

January 30, Rippon: "At University from 2 until 5. $13.75, dresses from Detroit."
January 30, Housel: "Came home this PM. Roads muddy."

Sunday January 31, Rippon: "Home Miss. [Missionary] sermon. Copied a little on St. Mark's. Will called. Read some of Daylight Land."
Sunday January 31, Housel: "Went to B. [Boulder]. M. [Mary]."

February 1, Rippon: "Perfect weather. Cloud effects fine. Faculty meeting 4–6, nothing accomplished."
February 1, Housel: "Went to B. [Boulder]. Worked butter."

February 2, Rippon: "Mrs. [Ida] Rosenkrans called."

February 3, Rippon: "Lecture on 'Lowell' by Oscar A. F. Greene at Mrs. [Emma] Wangelin's."

February 4, Rippon: "Snow. Extra Fortnightly. Mrs. Bowen and Mrs. Lockwood on program."
February 4, Housel: "Went to a lecture on Lowell last evening at Wangelins by O. [Oscar] A. F. Greene. M. [Mary]."

February 6, Rippon: "Snow quite deep. House noisy. Worked at Venice [lecture on Venice to be given to the Fortnightly Club]."
February 6, Housel: "Snowed hard all day. Cut locust posts, hauled manure."

Sunday February 7, Housel: "Went to B. [Boulder]. M. [Mary]."

February 8, Rippon: "Letters from Clara and Jeanne."
February 8, Housel: "Went for coal."

February 10, Housel: "Went to Farmers' Institute in Boulder."

February 11, Rippon: "Dr. [J. Raymond] Brackett's Opening of a Lotus Bud."

February 12, Rippon: "Tried my slides."
February 12, Housel: "Went up to Copper Rock. Located 'Trio' and its extension."

February 13, Rippon: "Wrote all day on Venice."

Sunday February 14, Rippon: "Wrote all day."
Sunday February 14, Housel: "Went to B. [Boulder]. Took Bell children [Rosetta, William, Cleophile, Geneva, and James] for a ride. M. [Mary]."

February 15, Rippon: "Went to Denver."
February 15, Housel: "Went to Denver. Warm."

February 16, Housel: "Came home this PM. Not much headway with the hard knot."

February 17, Rippon: "Came home."
February 17, Housel: "Worked at the stable. Went to B. [Boulder] this evening. Warm. M. [Mary]."

February 18, Rippon: "Worked on slides, rehearsal."

February 19, Rippon: "Venice evening [Mary's lecture and slide show to the Boulder Fortnightly Club]. Mrs. [Ida] Rosenkrans sent me roses."
February 19, Housel: "Went to B. [Boulder] to the Venice evening. Flailed beans. Cut trees."

February 20, Rippon: "Very tired. Caught severe cold at the 'contest' in the Rink."
February 20, Housel: "Flailed beans. Oratorical contest."

Sunday February 21, Rippon: "Slept all the morning. W. [Will] came. We went to see the Bells. Perfect day."
Sunday February 21, Housel: "M. [Mary]."

February 22, Rippon: "Was in Denver."
February 22, Housel: "Went to Gold Hill. Located the Hogback."

February 23, Rippon: "Heavy snow. Took hack [carriage]. Letter from Mason on alumni dinner."
February 23, Housel: "Snowstorm. Cleared off in PM. Went to town. M. [Mary]."

February 24, Rippon: "Hack. Day bright. De Long Bros. paid $530. Put it in bank. Paid church subscription in full."
February 24, Housel: "Cut trees in garden. Ed [Edgar Housel] lost a letter from Nice [probably regarding arrangements for Miriam who would soon be cared for in Nice, France]."

February 25, Rippon: "Fortnightly. Dr. [J. Raymond] Brackett talked to me."
February 25, Housel: "Went to B. [Boulder]. Money returned by Alumni Com. [Committee] in Denver. Father and wife [Louisa Bixby Wolcott Housel] went over to Lyman's. M. [Mary]"

February 26, Rippon: "Not very well. Mrs. Giffin called."
February 26, Housel: "Helped Ed [Edgar Housel] move press to Louisville."

February 27, "Fever. Sent for Dr. [Edwin] Hungerford. Lent Mr. [Henry] Rosenkrans $300."
February 27, Housel: "Went to Copper Rock."

Sunday February 28, Rippon: "Ill all day. W. [Will] came from mountains."
Sunday February 28, Housel: "Walked home via Sugar Loaf."

February 29, Rippon: "Out of school. Bad night."
February 29, Housel: "Went up to Copper Rock."

March 1, Rippon: "Better. Letter from Auntie [Hannah Skinner]."
March 1, Housel: "Worked on Trio [mine at Copper Rock]."

March 2, Rippon: "Mrs. Johnson called. She sent jelly and brown bread."
March 2, Housel: "Surveyed the Moly Hoses [mine at Copper Rock]."

March 3, Rippon: "Dr. [J. Raymond] Brackett and Mrs. [Delphine] Bell doing my work. Everyone kind."
March 3, Housel: "Began work on M. H. [Moly Hoses] on the [railroad] grade."

March 4, Rippon: "Head better. W. [Will] came."
March 4, Housel: "Came down home with Hawk Birch. Snowing. Walked out from B. [Boulder]."

March 5, Rippon: "Raining."
March 5, Housel: "Nursed my heel. Rain."

Sunday March 6, Rippon: "Snow."
Sunday March 6, Housel: "Do. [Nursed my heel, Rain.]"

March 7, Rippon: "Out again. One recitation. Mrs. Greene called."
March 7, Housel: "Drove Tops and Jean [horses] to C. R. [Copper Rock] and back."

March 8, Rippon: "2 recitations. Calls from Mrs. Smith and Thompson and Mrs. Dabny."
March 8, Housel: "Started the plow on S. E. corner of pasture. Ground in prime condition."

March 9, Rippon: "German courses in order. Light snow. Am gaining."
March 9, Housel: "Finished S. E. corner. Drove French, Selim and Roan [horses]. Snowed this morning. Cloudy all day and tonight."

March 10, Rippon: "Some headache. Could not attend Fortnightly. Pres. Eliott made us an address."
March 10, Housel: "Plowed N. E. corner of pasture in the holes, i.e., stone quarries."

March 11, Rippon: "Did all my recitation work. Too tired to attend Musicale at the [F. J.] Whitneys'."
March 11, Housel: "Finished the other side of creek and plowed on this side. Walter took hay to town."

March 12, Rippon: "Swept. Went to see Mrs. [Delphine] Bell. Drive with Mr. [Isaac] Dennett. Letter from Champaign about a position there."
March 12, Housel: "Plowed. Snowed."

Sunday March 13, Rippon: "Church, foggy. Will came."
Sunday March 13, Housel: "Went to B. [Boulder]. M. [Mary]."

March 14, Rippon: "Stormy. Did all my work. Letter from Helen B. [Beardsley]. Replied to K. L. Kennard, Champaign Ill."
March 14, Housel: "Hauled hay to barn."

March 15, Rippon: "Wrote Elizabeth. No calls except W. [Will]. Dr. [J. Raymond] Brackett brought photographs of sculptures."
March 15, Housel: "Went to town this evening."

March 16, Rippon: "Stormy and cold. Copied a little."

March 17, Rippon: "Colder. Below zero. Spent the evening with Mrs. [Delphine] Bell. Read part of Abeille."
March 17, Housel: "Snaked trees with Fan. [Fanny, Mary's horse]. Walter took hay to town."

March 18, Rippon: "No recitations. Wrote Mrs. [Annie] Culver. Cleaned student lamp inside. Letter from Jeanne. Wrote Mrs. [Mary] Welch."
March 18, Housel: "Fixed the coal house and the shop."

March 19, Rippon: "[Conrad] Bluhm won contest, 2nd place. Took tea at Bracketts."
March 19, Housel: "Cloudy and cold. Walter hauled manure. Jim [Housel] came. Ellets public sale. Took Fergusson home."

Sunday March 20, Rippon: "Sermon on Criminal Laws."
Sunday March 20, Housel: "Cold and cloudy all day. All stayed at home."

March 21, Rippon: "Look thru trunks. Went to University. Began Spanish in Testament. Went to Mrs. [Elizabeth] Mallons, played cards."
March 21, Housel: "Put a floor in the barn, east end."

March 22, Rippon: "Wrote Miriam. Cleaned silver. Calls from Mrs. Bowen and [Ida] Rosenkrans. Called on Mrs. Lowrie."
March 22, Housel: "Went to Copper Rock."

March 23, Rippon: "Wrote to Libbie [sister-in-law, wife of Omar Whitney]. Sent shirt. Blue lace. Brown silk-holder."
March 23, Housel: "Worked on Moly Hoses. Gold bugs tried to bluff us, then wanted an option."

March 24, Rippon: "Ripped green serge dress. Fortnightly."

March 24, Housel: "Gave an option on the Moly Hoses for $450 till April 17th."

March 25, Rippon: "Alumni Banquet in Denver. Wrote to Clara and to Jeanne. Ordered Little Minister for Jeanne."
March 25, Housel: "Plowed alfalfa grounds. Alumni Banquet in Denver tonight."

March 26, Rippon: "Read Stories of Venice with Mrs. [Ida] Rosenkrans."
March 26, Housel: "Took wheat up to clean. Hauled hay."

Sunday March 27, Rippon: "Sermon on Job. Drive with Will. Called on Gusta Anderson."
Sunday March 27, Housel: "Went to B. [Boulder]. Rode out with M. [Mary]."

March 28, Rippon: "Fine morning. School. Faculty meeting. Refused to pay assessment for decorating car to Colorado Springs. Wind."
March 28, Housel: "Plowed alfalfa."

March 29, Rippon: "Read with Mrs. [Ida] Rosenkrans in Stories of Venice."
March 29, Housel: "Do. [Plowed alfalfa] Took a load of clover hay to Baylor — 3250#."

March 30, Rippon: "Mrs. Bradley called. Carried photos to Mrs. Albee."
March 30, Housel: "Do. [Plowed alfalfa] With Jim [Housel]."

March 31, Rippon: "Letters from Libbie [sister-in-law] and Louella Gibbon. Read with Mrs. [Ida] R. [Rosenkrans]."
March 31, Housel: "Finished the old alfalfa and began the fallow-ground near the railroad."

April 1, Rippon: "Cold. Spent the evening at Mr. [Sidney A.] Giffin's."
April 1, Housel: "Harrowed. Jim [Housel] started the drill."

April 2, Rippon: "Mrs. White took me for a drive. Tea at Mrs. [Ida] Rosenkrans. Scientific meeting. Mr. Farnsworth had landscapes. Dr. [J. Raymond] Brackett Japanese drama."

Sunday April 3, Rippon: "Wrote to [former student] Mamie Johnson. Also to Helen B. [Beardsley]."
Sunday April 3, Housel: "Jim [Housel] and I went to see the Red Hill lode. Rained just before we got home."

April 4, Rippon: "Faculty meeting. Mrs. [Delphine] Bell went with me. Committee on examination. Tree planting."
April 4, Housel: "An inch of snow. Plowed S. of pasture."

April 5, Rippon: "Mrs. [Ida] R.[Rosenkrans] came to read 'Stories.'"
April 5, Housel: "Plowed and hauled hay."

April 6, Rippon: "Letter from Mrs. [Elizabeth] Wright. Frl. [Fraulein Hilda] Zulch read to me. Board meeting. Will came in late."
April 6, Housel: "Went to B. [Boulder] this evening. A pivotal point in Destiny."

April 7, Rippon: "Very warm. Read with Mrs. [Ida] R. [Rosenkrans]."
April 7, Housel: "Plowed beyond railroad."

April 8, Rippon: "A light snow."
April 8, Housel: "Got a new plow. Plowed do [beyond railroad]."

April 9, Rippon: "Denver high school students. Dinner at the varsity. Very tired."
April 9, Housel: "Plowed do [beyond railroad] AM. Got coal PM and went to B. [Boulder]. M[Mary]."

Sunday April 10, Rippon: "Sermon on mortality. A long walk with Will. Anemones. Mr. [Isaac] Dennett called. At two o'clock Col. [John] Ellet worse. Up the rest of the night."
Sunday April 10, Housel: "[Congregational] Church. [Reverend Charles] Caverno on mortality. Fine. Gathered anemones PM avec [with] M. [Mary]."

April 11, Rippon: "Col. [John] Ellet still worse. I did my work."
April 11, Housel: "Plowed on east side of railroad."

April 12, Rippon: "Col. [John] Ellet died at about 6 o'clock in the morning. Terrible day. I was at university."
April 12, Housel: "Jim [Housel] took hay to blacksmith. I drilled PM. Began raining about 5:30."

April 13, Rippon: "Put the house in order. Will came, took me for a drive. He stayed all night."
April 13, Housel: "An inch of snow. Jim [Housel] and I went to the butte [at Valmont]. Went to B. [Boulder] PM and stayed at the Ellet's."

April 14, Rippon: "Funeral at eleven o'clock. Dr. [John L.] Ellet, Mr. [R. C.] Jefferson, Mrs. Smith, Mr. Clinton and Mr. McIntyre came. Dr. [J. Raymond] Brackett came to take me home with him. Stayed all night. Will came to see me there."
April 14, Housel: "Col. Ellet's funeral at 11 AM. Took M. [Mary] for a ride this evening from Brackett's."

April 15, Rippon: "A quiet day at Dr. [J. Raymond] Brackett's. Tea with Mrs. [Lottie] Ellet. Night at Dr. [J. Raymond] Brackett's."

April 16, Rippon: "North and West Denver schools. Dinner at Mrs. Hankin's. Mr. [Isaac] Dennett called again. Letter from Mrs. [Annie] Culver."
April 16, Housel: "Went to Copper Rock PM. Drove Chief [horse]."

Sunday April 17, Rippon: "Easter. Immortality. Drive with W. [Will]."
Sunday April 17, Housel: "Came home. Went to B. [Boulder] M. [Mary]."

April 18, Rippon: "Letter from [former student] Helen B.[Beardsley]. Swept room. Storm began."
April 18, Housel: "Plowed PM till storm began. French [horse] died of colic."

April 19, Rippon: "Dr. J. L. Ellet left on early train. Mr. Jefferson on afternoon. Snowed all day."

April 19, Housel: "Heavy snow all day."

April 20, Rippon: "Snowed. Called at the [Sidney A.] Giffins'."
April 20, Housel: "Shelled corn. Went to B. [Boulder] evening."

April 21, Rippon: "Fortnightly. Tea with Mrs. Bowen."

April 22, Rippon: "Delta Gamma reception. Faculty meeting."

April 23, Rippon: "Drove with Mrs. Thompson. Called on Mrs. [Delphine] Bell and Mrs. Cullen."
April 23, Housel: "To Copper Rock. Worked on 'No Good' [mine]."

Sunday April 24, Rippon: "Law of wasted effort [sermon]. 'In the morning sow the seed and in the evening withhold not thy hand.'"
Sunday April 24, Housel: "Home again."

April 25, Rippon: "Drive with Will. Letters from Mrs. [Mary] Welch from Rome. Mrs. Norton, Mrs. [Elizabeth] Wright."
April 25, Housel: "Boulder. University. M. [Mary]."

April 26, Rippon: "Calls from Mrs. Bond, Nicholson, DeVris, Owen, Morath, Grill, Rogers. Began Viottetle Duc with Mrs. [Ida] Rosenkrans. Letters from Mme. F., Mr. Eliot."
April 26, Housel: "To Copper Rock."

April 27, Rippon: "Analyzed anemone. Grand Army parade. Read a little of le Duc. Letter from Miriam. Replied."
April 27, Housel: "Worked on No Good [mine]."

April 28, Rippon: "Frl. [Hilda] Zulch read Freitag's Life to me. Letter from MMC."
April 28, Housel: "Finished No Good, or Edna [mines]."

April 29, Rippon: "Mrs. E. in Denver. Remained with Mrs. Smith. Cut over stockings."
April 29, Housel: "Prospected on Orphan Boy Hill. Went to the Red Hill PM."

April 30, Rippon: "To Boulder Falls. Carried case of flowers to Dr. [J. Raymond] Brackett."
April 30, Housel: "Orphan Boy Hill AM. Located ambiguity PM. Came home."

Sunday May 1, Rippon: "Drove into country with Mrs. Smith. Sad. W. [Will] came. Wrote MMC."
Sunday May 1, Housel: "B. [Boulder] this evening. M. [Mary]."

May 2, Rippon: "Cloudy. Drove with W. [Will]. Talked of Germany."
May 2, Housel: "Plowed the pasture south of railroad."

May 3, Rippon: "Letter from Auntie [Hannah Skinner]. Emma Sternberg called. Card from [former student] Helen B. [Beardsley]."
May 3, Housel: "Do. [Plowed the pasture south of railroad]. Rain PM."

May 5, Rippon: "Fortnightly."
May 5, Housel: "Took [Valmont] butte rock to B. [Boulder]."

May 6, Rippon: "Party at Mrs. [Sidney A.] Giffin's."
May 6, Housel: "Seeded the lot. M. [Mary] in afternoon. About decided to go to Yale."

May 7, Rippon: "Rain all day. Snow."
May 7, Housel: "Trip to Gold Hill in a storm."

Sunday May 8, Rippon: "Church. Called on Mrs. [Lottie] Brackett. W. [Will] came."
Sunday May 8, Housel: "Snowed all night."

May 9, Rippon: "Called on Mrs. [Caroline] Greene. Looked at rooms. Mr. [Henry] R. [Rosenkrans] took [Luther] Beal note dated Feb. 6, 1891. Due in 10 months. $120 paid face $222. [Former student Timothy] Stanton came to see me."
May 9, Housel: "Cut and branded colts."

May 10, Rippon: "Calls from Mrs. Dabny, [Charles] Caverno, [Ida] Rosenkrans. Letter from Helen B. [Beardsley]."

May 10, Housel: "Went to B. [Boulder]. Bought the 25 acres from Father [Peter M. Housel], paying him $200 cash. Set locust trees PM."

May 11, Rippon: "Photo from Libbie of [nephew] Norman. Letter too. Wrote Fulton for [former student] Mamie Johnson. Wrote Helen B. [Beardsley]. W. [Will] came."
May 11, Housel: "Set out trees—locusts. Mack was down. Father [Peter M. Housel] and I went to Davidson's. Mr. Davidson sick. Went to B. [Boulder] in evening. M. [Mary]."

May 12, Rippon: "Mrs. Smith went with me to University. Beautiful photo of [nephew] Norman. Faculty meeting. Dr. [Isaac] Dennett called. Letter from Helen B. [Beardsley] Sent Helen $100."

May 12, Housel: "Set out trees, locusts and plums and raspberries."

May 13, Rippon: "Rain. Went to see Mrs. [Lottie] Brackett. Sent invitations for Wed. May 14, To Denver—bought hat, 'Tramp Abroad,' and candy. Helped Mrs. Gardiner in her shopping."

Sunday May 15, Rippon: "Church. W. [Will] came. Sunshine after 2 weeks of clouds and rain."
Sunday May 15, Housel: "Went to church. M. [Mary]."

May 16, Rippon: "Letter from France. M. [daughter Miriam] better. Rain. Faculty meeting. Did not go. Sent Helen $100. Dress from Detroit."
May 16, Housel: "Paid [Elijah] Autrey $300. The first note against the farm. Plowed, harrowed, etc. Jim [Housel] drilled and plowed."

May 17, Rippon: "Sent letter with $18.75 to Detroit. Social at Mrs. Williamson's."
May 17, Housel: "Went to B. [Boulder]. Left the deed to be recorded. Worked in garden."

May 18, Rippon: "Dr. [J. Raymond] Brackett and I had students in the evening. Mrs. Smith gave me roses."
May 18, Housel: "Plowed orchard, hauled hay. Worked in garden. Cultivated fruit, burnt brush, etc."

May 19, Rippon: "Fortnightly. Mrs. Smith went with me. Called on Miss Gamble."
May 19, Housel: "Drove Jet [horse]. Plowed orchard PM and set out bushes."

May 20, Rippon: "Philomalthean [Literary Society] Oration. [Wellie] Givens and [Henry] Andrew took prizes."
May 20, Housel: "Went to Denver. Drove Jean [horse] down. Cold NE wind all day."

May 21, Rippon: "Inauguration of President [James H.] Baker. Meeting of school superintendents and principals."
May 21, Housel: "Inauguration of [President James] Baker at University. Fine day."

Sunday May 22, Rippon: "Sermon on education by Mr. [Charles] Caverno. Fine sermon by Rev. Wm. Bayard Craig. [Recently widowed] Mrs. [Lizzie] Ellet left."
Sunday May 22, Housel: "Perfect day. Baccalaureate sermon by William Bayard Craig. — 'Ask, give, serve.' Good."

May 23, Rippon: "Alone in the [Ellet] house. Did not go to Bell Lit.[Literary Society]. Dance in the evening."
May 23, Housel: "Bac. [Baccalaureate]."

May 24, Rippon: "At University to register ranks, etc. Mrs. [Ida] Rosenkrans called. Heavy rain. W. [Will] came. Did not hear [Rev.] Myron Reed."
May 24, Housel: "Didn't go to hear [Rev.] Myron Reed."

May 25, Rippon: "Class day. Fine weather. Faculty meeting."
May 25, Housel: "Went to Copper Rock."

May 26, Rippon: "Commencement. Fine weather. Dinner at the Bowen [Hotel]. Bad. Alumni exercises in the evening."
May 26, Housel: "Commencement Day. Alumni Banquet. Exercises and business meeting."

May 27, Rippon: "Tired. Helped Mrs. [Jennie] Baker arrange flowers. [President's] reception very pretty. Appointed on committee at Fortnightly."

May 27, Housel: "Wrote up banquet for *Herald* and alumni exercises for *Republican*. President Baker's reception."

May 28, Rippon: "Will came for me to drive. Mr. [Isaac] Dennett came in the evening."

Sunday May 29, Rippon: "Attended church. W. [Will] came."

May 30, Rippon: "Packed some. Dr. [J. Raymond] Brackett and W. [Will] boxed my books."

May 31, Rippon: "Very tired. Left the Ellet house. Attended Fortnightly banquet. Slept at Dr. [J. Raymond] Brackett's house. Rain."

May 31, Housel: "Went to Denver."

June 1, Rippon: "Trunks moved. Arranged new room."

June 1, Housel: "Went to B. [Boulder]. Frost."

June 2, Rippon: "Read with Mrs. [Ida] R. [Rosenkrans]."

June 2, Housel: "Drove up to Copper Rock."

June 3, Rippon: "To Gold Hill. Lots of flowers. Grand views."

June 3, Housel: "Myrtle's colt came this morning—sorrel, horse. Went to B. [Boulder]. M.[Mary] went to Gold Hill. Irrigated trees."

June 4, Rippon: "Rain. Read with Mrs. [Ida] R.[Rosenkrans]."

June 4, Housel: "Irrigated trees. Rain from 9 on."

Sunday June 5, Rippon: "Sermon on Jonah. Will came to tea. Walked to University for books."

Sunday June 5, Housel: "Got letters from Janesville and from Denver. Went to B. [Boulder] PM and over to the University. Go to Denver in morning. M. [Mary]."

June 6, Rippon: "At Univ. with Mrs. [Ida] R. [Rosenkrans] Wrote to Mrs. [Lizzie] Ellet. Ride on horseback with Mr. [Isaac] Dennett."
June 6, Housel: "Went to Denver and on to Ft. Collins in the evening."

June 7, Rippon: "At University. Dr. [J. Raymond] Brackett left. Card from Helen [Beardsley] dated Munich, May 25. Wrote to Chicago for Helen."
June 7, Housel: "Wool Growers Convention in Agricultural Hall."

June 8, Rippon: "Calls from Misses Maxwell, Sternberg, and Andrews. Made garden beds."
June 8, Housel: "Field Day sports. Subscription money starting to come in."

June 9, Rippon: "Called on Miss Johnson."
June 9, Housel: "Commencement Day at [Fort] Collins. Hot."

June 10, Rippon: "Washed. Mrs. [Ida] R. [Rosenkrans] came. Mrs. [Emma] Wangelin offered me a room."
June 10, Housel: "Rustled about."

June 11, Rippon: "Tired. Mrs. [Delphine] Bell came with news of Mrs. McGraw's attempt at suicide."

Sunday June 12, Rippon: "Children's day. Went twice to [Congregational Church] service."
Sunday June 12, Housel: "Bred Myrtle. From Collins to B. [Boulder] and back in evening."

June 13, Rippon: "Mrs. Walker and Mrs. Hutchinson came to see pressed flowers. Ironed one large curtain. Read."

June 14, Rippon: "Mrs. Albee called. Tramp with Willie [Will Brackett, 8 year-old son of Lottie and J. Raymond Brackett] to Sunshine Canon. Read a little."

June 15, Rippon: "Ironed one curtain. W. [Will] came. Funeral of Rollins Brown. Thirty dollars to Miriam."
June 15, Housel: "Down to Boulder in morning and on to Denver PM."

June 16, Rippon: "Excursion to Greeley."
June 16, Housel: "Work in office."

June 17, Rippon: "Began Life of Columbus at Mrs. [Sidney A.] Giffin's. 15 ladies present."
June 17, Housel: "Office work. Papers drawn up."

June 18, Rippon: "Washed black and white shawl. Drive with Ed [Edgar] Housel. Read with Mrs. [Ida] R. [Rosenkrans]. Dr. B. [Brackett] ret. [returned] from trip south."
June 18, Housel: "To Ft. Collins AM. Signed papers before leaving Denver."

Sunday June 19, Rippon: "W. [Will] came. Dined at Pres. [James H.] Baker's. Gave Will $600 to pay on Colorado Farmer."
Sunday June 19, Housel: "Down to B. [Boulder]. M.[Mary] during church. Out home. Rented a room of Mrs. Cullin at $3.00 a month. Paid one month in advance."

June 20, Rippon: "At Univ. Rode with Mrs. [Jennie] Baker."
June 20, Housel: "Worked on reservoir data."

June 21, Rippon: "Mrs. Johnson called. Looked over photos of Greek sculpture."
June 21, Housel: "Ditto [reservoir data] to finish. Went home with Pennock."

June 22, Rippon: "With Mr. Jefferson and Mrs. Cullen to Bo. [Boulder] Falls."
June 22, Housel: "Wrote up P. and others. Four subs.[subscriptions for Colorado Farmer]. One ad."

June 23, Rippon: "Read with Mrs. B. Analyzed 4 flowers. Read at Mrs. Giffin's."

June 23, Housel: "To Greeley for commencement and back to [Fort] Collins."

BIBLIOGRAPHY

Introduction
Magazine references include:

- McClurg, Kathy. "Mary, Mary, Extraordinary." *Summit* Magazine, Winter 1987, page 13.
- Staff. "Alum Donates Brackett Originals." *Colorado Alumnus*, Volume 66 #7, February 1976, page 3.

Part I: Early Years, 1850–1877
Chapter 1
Author's site visits include:

- Thomas F. Rippon's grave, June 26, 1998. Lot 315, Lisbon Cemetery, Lisbon, Kendall County, Illinois.

Book references include:

- Staff. *Portrait and Biographical Album of Livingston County, Illinois.* Chapman Brothers, 1888, page 268.

Census references include:

- U.S. Census, Lisbon Township, Kendall County, Illinois, 1850.

Courthouse records include:

- Thomas F. Rippon Final Certificate No. 21336. General Land Entry Files, April 10, 1847, National Archives.

- Thomas F. Rippon probate records. April 24, 1851, Kendall County Circuit Court, Kendall County, Illinois.

Unpublished material and manuscripts include:

- Rippon, Mary. Notations for the Carnegie Retirement fund, 1909. Archives, University of Colorado at Boulder Libraries, Mary Rippon collection.

Chapter 2
Book references include:

- First General Assembly. *Revised Statutes of the State of Illinois.* Illinois General Assembly, Springfield, Illinois, 1845, pages 201, 535, 545–546.

Census references include:

- U.S. Bureau of the Census. "Historical Statistics of the U.S.," Government Printing Office, Washington, D.C., 1975.
- U.S. Bureau of the Census, "Statistical Abstracts of the U.S.," Government Printing Office, Washington, D.C., 1997.
- U.S. Census. Lisbon Township, Kendall County, Illinois. 1860.

Courthouse records include:

- Henry and George Kellogg and William W. Skinner mortgage records. Book R, 275–280, November 25, 1856. Kendall County Clerk and Recorder, Kendall County, Illinois.
- Mary Ann Rippon guardianship records, April 25, 1853, April 11, 1855, January 7, 1857, and February 28, 1857. Kendall County Circuit Court, Kendall County, Illinois.
- N. W. Whitney and Jane Rippon marriage records. Book A, 50, September 1, 1853, Kendall County Clerk and Recorder, Kendall County, Illinois.
- Norman W. Whitney land records. Book L, 54, June 27, 1853, Kendall County Clerk and Recorder, Kendall County, Illinois.

- Thomas F. Rippon probate records, April 24, 1851, May 18, 1851; and Bill of Appraisement, 1851. Kendall County Circuit Court, Kendall County, Illinois.
- William W. Skinner "Guardian of Mary Ann Rippon, vs. Jane Whitney and Norman Whitney," Petition for Dower, June 13, 1856 and October 4, 1856. Kendall County Circuit Court, Kendall County, Illinois.

Newspaper references include:

- Staff. "Whitney Is Dead." *Topeka Capital Journal*, August 31, 1925.

Chapter 3
Author's interviews include:

- Thomas Fletcher, Sr., June 25, 1998.

Book references include:

- Farren, Kathy. *A Bicentennial History of Kendall County, Illinois*. Kendall County Bicentennial Commission, 1976, pages 142, 151.
- Lawyer, Marvin L. *The Old Rural Schools of Kendall County*. Marvin L. Lawyer, 1995, pages 293–294.

Census references include:

- U.S. Census, Lisbon Township, Kendall County, Illinois, 1860.

Courthouse records include:

- Mary Ann Rippon guardianship records, October 10, 1857, October 6, 1858, and March 18, 1869, Kendall County Circuit Court, Kendall County, Illinois.
- William Skinner and Hannah Alford marriage records. Book A, 100, December 12, 1861, Kendall County Clerk and Recorder, Kendall County, Illinois.

Chapter 4
Author's interviews include:

- Telephone conversation with Roger Platt (Illinois Regional Archives Depository intern). Illinois State University, November 28, 1995.

Book and magazine references include:

- McClurg, Kathy. "Mary, Mary Extraordinary." *Summit* Magazine, Winter 1987, page 12.
- Mumey, Nolie. "Joseph Addison Sewall, 1830–1917, Pioneer, Physician, Educator, and the First President of the University of Colorado." *The* Westerners Brand Book, 1966, Johnson Publishing Company, 1967, pages 93–107.
- State Normal University. *Catalogue of State Normal University for the Academic Year Ending June 26, 1868.* Steam-Power Book and Job Printing House, 1868.
- Thompson, Eleanor Wolf. *Education for Ladies 1830–1960.* Kings Crown Press, 1947, page 93.
- Woody, Thomas. *A History of Women's Education in the United States*, Volume I. The Science Press, 1929, pages 333, 483.

Census references include:

- U.S. Bureau of the Census. "Historical Statistics of the U.S.," Government Printing Office, Washington, D.C., 1975.
- U.S. Bureau of the Census. "Statistical Abstracts of the U.S.," Government Printing Office, Washington, D.C, 1997.

Courthouse records include:

- Mary Rippon guardianship records, January 1864, Kendall County Circuit Court, Kendall County, Illinois.

Newspaper references include:

- Classified advertisement. "Morris Advertiser." August 26, 1865.

- Staff. "The University of Colorado, Its Origin and Development." Boulder *Daily Camera*, March 1, 1912.
- Staff. "First President of the University and His Family Lived in Old Main During Early Days of the School." Boulder *Daily* Camera, undated clipping (circa 1950).

Unpublished material and manuscripts include:

- Pillsbury, William I., Letter of recommendation written for Mary Rippon, November 28, 1867. Archives, University of Colorado at Boulder Libraries, Mary Rippon collection.
- Rippon, Mary, Account book, 1916–1926. Archives, University of Colorado at Boulder Libraries. Mary Rippon collection.

Chapter 5
Author's interviews include:

- Telephone conversation with Julia Frey (associate professor of French, University of Colorado), November 28, 1995.

Book and magazine references include:

- Clarke, Edward H. *Sex in Education, A Fair Chance for Girls.* Boston, 1873.
- Cott, Nancy F., and Elizabeth H. Pleck. *A Heritage of Her Own, Toward a New Social History of American Women.* Simon and Schuster, 1979, page 131.
- Hanaford, Phebe A. *Daughters of America, or Women of the Century.* Augusta, Maine, 1882.
- Howe, Julia Ward, editor. *Sex and Education: A Reply to Dr. E. H. Clarke's Sex In Education.* Roberts Brothers, 1874, page 7.
- *Leading Industries of the West.* Chicago: H. S. Reed & Co., 1883, page 51.
- McClurg, Kathy. "Mary, Mary Extraordinary." *Summit* Magazine, Winter 1987, page 12.
- Solberg, Winton U. *The University of Illinois, 1867–1894, An Intellectual and Cultural History.* University of Illinois Press, 1968, page 160.

Census references include:

- U.S. Bureau of the Census. "Historical Statistics of the U.S. Government Printing Office," 1975.
- U.S. Bureau of the Census, "Statistical Abstracts of the U.S. Government Printing Office," 1997.

Courthouse records include:

- Mary Ann Rippon Guardianship Records, March 18, 1869. Kendall County Circuit Court, Kendall County, Illinois.

Genealogical records include:

- Mary Rippon Passport application number 7409, June 18, 1883. National Archives.

Newspaper references include:

- Staff. "Barstow-Massey wedding." *Morris Herald Advertiser*, August 3, 1872.
- Staff. "Miss Mary Rippon Was a Large Part of the U. of C." Boulder Daily Camera, November 4, 1927.
- Uncited clipping, "Varsity." April 11, 1885, Archives, University of Colorado at Boulder Libraries, James Washington Bell collection.
- Undated and uncited clipping. "Learning German at Hannover." Archives, University of Colorado at Boulder Libraries, Mary Rippon collection.

Unpublished material and manuscripts include:

- Mrs. Norlin's papers. Archives, University of Colorado at Boulder Libraries, George Norlin collection.
- Rippon, Mary, to Annie (Anna von Brandis) correspondence, December 1874. Archives, University of Colorado at Boulder Libraries, Mary Rippon collection.

- Sewall, Joseph A., to Mary Rippon correspondence, August 3, 1877. Archives, University of Colorado at Boulder Libraries, Mary Rippon collection.

Part II: **Single Years, 1878–1887**
Chapter 6
Book and magazine references include:

- Allen, Frederick S., et al. *The University of Colorado 1876–1976.* Harcourt Brace Jovanovich, 1976, page 39.
- Bixby, Amos. "Little Journeys in the Year One." *Coloradoan*, Volume IV. University of Colorado, 1903, page 17.
- Jackson, Helen Hunt. *Bits of Travel at Home.* Roberts Brothers, 1878.
- Jackson, Helen Hunt. "The Procession of Flowers in Colorado," *Atlantic Monthly*, October 1877.
- Staff. "Miss Mary Rippon, Former Instructor in Colorado." *Colorado Alumnus,* Volume XVIII, February 1928, page 4.

Census references include:

- U.S. Bureau of the Census, "Historical Statistics of the U.S.," Government Printing Office, 1975.
- U.S. Bureau of the Census, "Statistical Abstracts of the U.S.," Government Printing Office, 1997.

Newspaper references include:

- Staff. "Old Main Declared Safe." *Boulder County News*, July 6, 1877.
- Staff. "Joseph Sewall." *Boulder County News*, October 26, 1877.
- Staff. "Miss Mary Rippon Was a Large Part of the U. of C." Boulder *Daily* Camera, November 4, 1927.
- Staff. "Mary Rippon, Pioneer U. C. Teacher Dies." Boulder *Daily* Camera, September 9, 1935.

Unpublished material and manuscripts include:

- Sewall, Joseph A., to Mary Rippon correspondence, 1877 (October 10 and December 11). Archives, University of Colorado at Boulder Libraries, Mary Rippon collection.
- University of Colorado Regents' Minutes. "Mary to Start Teaching on 7 January 1878," June 29, 1878, 14.

Chapter 7
Book and magazine references include:

- Bixby, Amos. "Little Journeys in the Year One." *Coloradoan*, Volume IV. University of Colorado, 1903, pages 15, 17.
- Staff. *Leading Industries of the West.* Chicago: H. S. Reed & Co., 1883, pages 49–50.
- Staff. "Miss Mary Rippon, Former Instructor in Colorado." *Colorado Alumnus,* Volume XVIII, University of Colorado, February 1928, page 4.

Newspaper references include:

- Staff. *Boulder* County News, September 7, 1877, February 1, 1878, and June 7, 1878.

Unpublished material and manuscripts include:

- Ricketts, Elizabeth. Oral History Tape #190, March 10, 1975. Carnegie Branch Library for Local History, Boulder, Colorado.

Chapter 8
Book and magazine references include:

- Allen, Frederick S., et al. *The University of Colorado 1876–1976.* Harcourt Brace Jovanovich, 1976, page 30.
- Bixby, Amos. "Little Journeys in the Year One." *Coloradoan*, Volume IV. University of Colorado, 1903, page 14.
- Staff. "Remarks of Dr. Stanton." *Colorado Alumnus,* Volume XXVII. University of Colorado, December 1936, pages 5–7.

- Staff. *University of Colorado Announcement, 1877–1878*. University of Colorado, 1878.
- Staff. *University* Portfolio, Volume I #1. University of Colorado, December 1879.
- Woody, Thomas. *A History of Women's Education in the United States*, Volume II. The Science Press, 1929, page 327.

Genealogical records include:

- Rippon, Mary, Passport application number 7409. June 18, 1883, National Archives.

Newspaper references include:

- Staff. *Boulder* County News. January 14, 1876, and January 25, 1878.
- Staff. *Boulder* News *and* Courier. June 16, 1882.
- Staff. *Denver* Tribune, January 18, 1880.
- Staff. *Rocky* Mountain News, October 18, 1879.
- Staff. "Edgar S. Housel, Boulder Pioneer, Dies in Michigan." Boulder *Daily Camera*, April 22, 1952.

Chapter 9
Book and magazine references include:

- Allen, Frederick S., et al, *The University of Colorado 1876–1976*. Harcourt Brace Jovanovich, 1976, page 39.
- Bartlett, Albert A., John A. Brennan, and John K. Emery. "One Hundred Years Ago." Centennial Committee of the College of Arts and Sciences of the University of Colorado, 1982, page 12.
- Rothman, Sheila. *Woman's Proper Place: A History of Changing Ideals and Practices 1870 to the Present*. Basic Books, 1978, page 23.
- Staff. *University* Portfolio, Volume I #4. University of Colorado, June 1880.
- Staff. *University* Portfolio, Volume III #5. University of Colorado. June 1882.

- Staff. "From Cactus Field to University Campus." *Colorado* Alumnus, Volume XXV, University of Colorado, June 1935, page 5.

Census references include:

- U.S. Bureau of the Census, "Historical Statistics of the U.S.," Government Printing Office, 1975.
- U.S. Bureau of the Census, "Statistical Abstracts of the U.S.," Government Printing Office, 1997.

Newspaper references include:

- Staff. *Boulder* County Herald Weekly. September 8, 1880.
- Staff. *Boulder* News *and* Courier. June 9, 1882.
- Staff. *Colorado* Banner. June 19, 1879.

Unpublished material and manuscripts include:

- Hale, Horace M., to Mary Rippon correspondence. May 23, 1881. Archives, University of Colorado at Boulder Libraries, Mary Rippon collection.
- Rippon, Mary, diary, January 9, 1883, and March 16, 1892. Archives, University of Colorado at Boulder Libraries, Mary Rippon collection.

Chapter 10
Unpublished material and manuscripts include:

- Passenger lists of the S.S. *Austral*. August 18, 1884, National Archives.
- Pease, Ernest, to Minnie Adams correspondence, 1884 (May 31 to June 11, July 11, July 19), Archives, University of Colorado at Boulder Libraries, Ernest Pease collection.
- Rippon, Mary Rippon, 1883 (March 23, April 19, May 20, June 14–25, July 2–August 6, October 8–November 4). Archives, University of Colorado at Boulder Libraries, Mary Rippon collection.
- Rippon, Mary, diary, 1884 (July 22–24). Archives, University of Colorado at Boulder Libraries, Mary Rippon collection.

Chapter 11
Book and magazine references include:

- Sewall, Jane. *Jane Dear Child.* University of Colorado Press, 1957, page 40.
- Staff. *University* Portfolio, Volume VI #1. October 1884.

Census references include:

- Colorado Census, 1885.

Newspaper references include:

- Rippon, Mary. "An Interesting History of the Fortnightly Club." Boulder Daily Camera, May 27, 1930.
- Staff. *Boulder* County Herald Weekly, July 16, 1884 and February 11, 1885.
- Staff. *Boulder* News *and* Courier. August 24, 1883.
- Staff. "Boulder Women and Their Club." The *Denver Sunday Times,* December 17, 1899.
- Staff. "Dean J. R. Brackett Dies Here Sunday." Boulder Daily Camera, July 10, 1922.
- Staff. "Varsity" (uncited clipping). April 11, 1885, Archives, University of Colorado at Boulder Libraries, James Washington Bell collection.

Unpublished material and manuscripts include:

- Rippon, Mary, diary, December 12, 1884. Archives, University of Colorado at Boulder Libraries, Mary Rippon collection.
- University of Colorado Regents' Minutes. September 29, 1883.
- Wangelin, Emma, to Mary Rippon correspondence. August 3, 1920.

Chapter 12
Author's interviews include:

- Telephone conversation with Hope Lynch (archivist, Delta Gamma Executive Office), November 28, 1995.

Book and magazine references include:

- Allen, Frederick S. *The University of Colorado 1876–1976.* Harcourt Brace Jovanovich, 1976, pages 33, 47, 270.
- Davis, William E. Glory Colorado, The History of the University of Colorado, 1858–*1963.* Pruett Press, 1965, page 54.
- Delta Gamma, Anchora, March 1887.
- Sewall, Joseph A. "Quarto-Centennial Celebration, University of Colorado." *University* of Colorado Bulletin Number II, December 1902, page 103.
- Staff. "Dedication of the Theater," *Colorado Alumnus,* Volume XXVII. December 1936, page 5.
- Staff. *University of Colorado Catalogue,* 1877–*1878.* Archives, University of Colorado at Boulder Libraries.

Newspaper references include:

- Staff. "First President of the University and His Family Lived in Old Main During Early Days of the School." Boulder *Daily* Camera, undated article ca. 1950s.

Unpublished material and manuscripts include:

- Letter of recommendation regarding Mary Rippon from Joseph A. Sewall, May 3, 1887. Archives, University of Colorado at Boulder Libraries, Mary Rippon collection.

Part 3: Hidden Years, 1887–1893
Chapter 13
Book and magazine references include:

- Bixby, Amos. "Little Journeys in the Year One." *Coloradoan,* Volume IV. University of Colorado, 1903, page 17.
- von Goethe, Johann Wolfgang. *Faust.* W. W. Norton & Co., 1976, page 35 (lines 1449–1470).

- Staff. *University* of Colorado General Record 1877–*1892.* Archives, University of Colorado at Boulder Libraries.
- Staff. *University of Colorado Catalogue,* 1879–*1880 and 1888–1889*. Archives, University of Colorado at Boulder Libraries.

Unpublished material and manuscripts include:

- Housel, William Cephas. Passport application number 3616, June 1889. National Archives.
- Pease, Ernest M. "Boyhood of E. M. Pease." Carnegie Branch Library for Local History, Boulder, Colorado, 1933, pages 58–59.
- Rippon, Mary, diary, April 6, 1885. Archives, University of Colorado at Boulder Libraries, Mary Rippon collection.
- Rippon, Mary, diary, loose undated page.

Chapter 14

Book and magazine references include:

- Faragher, John Mack, and Florence Howe. *Women and Higher Education in American History.* Norton & Co., 1988, pages xv, 173.
- Kellogg, Dr. J. H. *Ladies' Guide in Health and Disease.* W. D. Condit & Co., 1883, pages 323, 300–331.

Courthouse records include:

- William C. Housel and Mary Rippon, Marriage application and certificate #27812, June 9, 1888. Recorder of Deeds, St. Louis, Missouri.

Newspaper references include:

- Staff. *Rocky* Mountain News, May 3, 1888.
- Staff. *Boulder* County Herald Weekly, June 6, 1888.
- Walker, Dr. H. H. "Divorce, A Sermon by Dr. H. H. Walker." Boulder *Daily* Camera, April 5, 1906.

Chapter 15

Author's interviews include:

- Roland Wolcott, July 19, 1995, and August 7, 1995. (In reference to Mary and Will's marriage and the birth of Miriam, Roland Wolcott related that his sister Evelyn Wolcott once told him, "We knew about it, but didn't talk about it.")

Book and magazine references include:

- Chapman Brothers. *Portrait and Biographical Album of Livingston County, Illinois.* Chapman Brothers, 1888, page 268.
- Staff. *University* Portfolio, Volume VII #1, February 1889.
- Wertz, Richard W., and Dorothy C. Wertz, *Lying-In: A History of Childbirth in America.* Free Press, 1977, page 80.

Newspaper references include:

- Staff. *Boulder* County Herald Weekly. July 25, 1888 and January 9, 1889.
- Staff. "Death of W.W. Skinner." *Fairbury Blade.* September 22, 1888.
- Staff. "James Washington Bell." *Sentinel.* January 10, 1890.
- Staff. "Norman R. Whitney." *Topeka Capital Journal.* December 10, 1963.
- Staff. "Mrs. Miriam Rieder Dies After Long Illness Thursday." Boulder Daily Camera, September 27, 1957.

Unpublished material and manuscripts include:

- Bell, Rosetta, Autograph book, 1889. Archives, University of Colorado at Boulder Libraries, Rosetta Bell Wolcott collection.
- Graceland Cemetery records. Dominy Memorial Library, Fairbury, Illinois.
- News Bureau form, Public Relations Department. University of Colorado, 1953, Miriam Rieder file.
- Rieder, Miriam, Passport application. August 23, 1916. National Archives.

- Rieder, Miriam Edna Housel, Social Security account application. October 25, 1955, Social Security Administration.
- Rieder, Miriam, Death Certificate. September 27, 1957, Colorado Department of Health, vital records.
- University of Colorado, Regents' Minutes, July 21, 1888.
- University Portfolio, Volume VII #1, February 1889.

Chapter 16

Author's site visits include:

- Graceland Cemetery, Fairbury, Illinois, June 26, 1998.

Book and magazine references include:

- Staff. *University* Portfolio, Volume VII #3. May 1889.

Newspaper references include:

- Staff. *Boulder County Herald Weekly,* May 22 and 29, 1889, June 12, 1889, and August 14, 1889.
- Staff. *Boulder News*, May 23 and 30, 1889.

Unpublished material and manuscripts include:

- Housel, William Cephas, Passport application number 3616, June 1889. National Archives.
- Passenger lists, SS *Belgenland*, August 16, 1889. National Archives.
- University of Colorado. University of Colorado Catalogue, 1888–1889.

Chapter 17

Author interviews include:

- Correspondence with Dr. Ross Ingersoll, September 10, 1997.

Book and magazine references include:

- Bible of Peter M. Housel, in possession of Edgar Searles Housel.

- von Goethe, Johann Wolfgang. *Faust.* W. W. Norton & Co., 1976, pages 27 (lines 1112–1117).
- McClurg, Kathy. "Mary, Mary, Extraordinary." *Summit* Magazine (Winter 1987), page 13.
- Staff. Catalogue and Announcements of the University of Colorado and State Preparatory School, 1891–1892. Archives, University of Colorado at Boulder Libraries.
- Staff. *Directory of Officers and Graduates*, 1877–1921. University of Colorado Bulletin, Volume XXI #10, General Series #175, 1921.
- Staff. *University* Portfolio, Volumes VIII–IX, 1889–1891. Archives, University of Colorado at Boulder Libraries.

Courthouse records include:

- Diantha Skinner, death records, Book 1, 68; November 16, 1890. Kendall County Clerk and Recorder, Kendall County, Illinois.

Newspaper references include:

- Rippon, Mary. "An Interesting History of the Fortnightly Club." Boulder Daily Camera, May 27, 1930.
- Staff. "Miss Rippon Returned to Boulder Friday Morning." *Boulder* County Herald Weekly, September 9, 1891.
- Staff. *Boulder* County Herald Weekly, November 13, 1889.
- Staff. *Boulder* News, January 2, 1890, May 15, 1890, and May 7, 1891.
- Staff. *Rocky* Mountain News, November 16, 1889.
- Staff. *Sentinel*, January 10, 1890.
- Staff. "Views of the Legislators" (uncited clipping), February 27, 1891. Archives, University of Colorado in Boulder Libraries, Mary Rippon collection.
- *Unpublished* material and manuscripts include:
- Bell, Delphine, scrapbook, in possession of Roland Wolcott.
- Housel, William, diploma, University of Leipzig, March 18, 1890, in possession of Robert P. Housel.

- Rieder, Miriam, *Grasp* That Torch (undated, unpublished manuscript). Archives, University of Colorado at Boulder Libraries, Miriam Rieder collection.
- Rippon, Mary, diary, January 17, 1890. Archives, University of Colorado at Boulder Libraries, Mary Rippon collection.
- Rippon, Mary, diary, loose undated page circa 1890/1891, Archives, University of Colorado at Boulder Libraries, Mary Rippon collection.
- Rippon, Mary, diary, loose undated page ca. 1890/1891.
- Rippon, Mary, diary, accounting section, 1892.
- Stalker, Jean Bentley, "History of the Peter M. Housel Family as Related by a Granddaughter" (unsigned, undated, and unpublished manuscript). Carnegie Branch Library for Local History, Boulder, Colorado.
- Université de Genève, "Livret d'Etudiant," W. C. Housel, in possession of Robert P. Housel.
- Wescott, Lois, compiler, *Boulder* County Colorado Estate Files, 1862–1904 (unpublished manuscript). Carnegie Branch Library for Local History, Boulder, Colorado.
- Wolcott, Frank H., to "Gov." Paddock, March 6, 1959. Boulder *Daily* Camera files.

Chapter 18

Book and magazine references include:

- Greene, Harvey. *The Light of the Home: An Intimate View of the Lives of Women in Victorian America*. Pantheon Books, 1983.

Newspaper references include:

- Rippon, Mary. "An Interesting History of the Fortnightly Club." Boulder Daily Camera, May 27, 1930.
- Staff. Boulder County News, July 2, 1875.
- Staff. *Boulder* Herald Weekly, December 16, 1891.
- Staff. *Boulder* News, December 17, 1891.
- Staff. *Boulder* County Herald Weekly, January 27, 1892 and April 20, 1892.

- Staff. "Miss Rippon's Lecture." *Boulder County Herald Weekly*, February 24, 1892.

Unpublished material and manuscripts include:

- Housel, Will, diary, 1892 (February 16 and March 17), in possession of Robert P. Housel.
- Rippon, Mary, diary, 1892 (January 1 and 17, February 21, April 14, and May 16). Archives, University of Colorado at Boulder Libraries, Mary Rippon collection.

Chapter 19
Newspaper references include:

- Staff. *Boulder* County Herald Weekly, June 15, 1892.

Unpublished material and manuscripts include:

- Housel, Will, diary, 1892. (March 14), in possession of Robert P. Housel.
- Kennard, Katherine L., to Mary Rippon. March 9, 1892. Archives, University of Colorado at Boulder Libraries, Mary Rippon collection.
- Rippon, Mary, to Katherine L. Kennard. March 14, 1892. Archives, University of Colorado at Boulder Libraries, Mary Rippon collection.
- Rieder, Miriam. Passport application, August 23, 1916, with accompanying letter of August 22, 1916, National Archives.
- Rippon, Mary, diary, 1892 (March 12, June 19, August 29, September 4, and October 4). Archives, University of Colorado at Boulder Libraries, Mary Rippon collection.
- Rippon, Mary, diary, accounting sections, 1892 and 1893. Archives, University of Colorado at Boulder Libraries, Mary Rippon collection.

Chapter 20
Author's interviews include:

- Correspondence with Becca Marinelli (Catholic Charities and Community Services, Lakewood, Colorado), April 26, 1995.

Book and magazine references include:

- Ives, Prof. Halsey C. *The Dream City: A Portfolio of Photographic Views of the World's Columbian Exposition.* N. D. Thompson Publishing Co., 1893.
- Kunitz, Stanley J., and Howard Haycraft. *American Authors, 1600–1900: A Biographical Dictionary of American Literature.* H. W. Wilson Co., 1938.
- Lawson, James Gilchrist, editor. *The World's Best Loved Poems.* Harper & Row, 1927, pages 150–151.
- Staff. *Columbine*, Volume I. Homerian Literary Society of the University of Colorado, May 1, 1893, page 41.
- Staff. *Silver* and Gold, Volume I #23, March 1893.
- Staff. *Silver* and Gold, Volume I #32, May 16, 1893.
- Staff. *University of Michigan Catalogue of Graduates, Non-Graduates, Officers, and Members of the Faculties.* University of Michigan Press, 1923.

Newspaper references include:

- Staff. "Divorce, A Sermon by Dr. H. H. Walker." Boulder *Daily Camera*, April 5, 1906.
- Staff. Boulder *Daily* Camera, May 7, 1893.

Unpublished material and manuscripts include:

- Rippon, Mary, diary, 1893 (May 23, June 18–22, July 3–5, and December 26). Archives, University of Colorado at Boulder Libraries, Mary Rippon collection.
- Rippon, Mary. Account book, 1900. Archives, University of Colorado at Boulder Libraries, Mary Rippon collection.

Courthouse records include

- Housel, Will, land records, 1893, Books 157 and 158. Boulder County Clerk and Recorder, Boulder, Colorado.

Part 4: Separate Years, 1893–1909
Chapter 21
Author's interviews include:

- Joy Whitney Ahlborn, July 7, 1995.

Book and magazine references include:

- Davis, William E. *Glory* Colorado. Pruett Press, 1965, page 111.
- Kinder, Francis S., and F. Clarence Spencer. *Evenings With Colorado Poets: A Compilation of Selections from Colorado Poets and Verse-Writers.* Chain and Hardy Company, 1894.
- Staff. "In the Beginning," *Coloradoan*, Volume V. University of Colorado, 1904, pages 13–26.
- Staff. *The Ladies Home Journal,* Volume XVI #10." September 1899, page 16.

Courthouse records include:

- Housel, William Cephas, and Dora Mae Searles, Certificate of Marriage, Register #11490-96. July 16, 1896, Borough of Manhattan, New York, New York.
- Rippon, Mary, land records, 1895, Book 176. Boulder County Clerk and Recorder, Boulder, Colorado.

Newspaper references include:

- Rippon, Mary. "An Interesting History of the Fortnightly Club." Boulder *Daily* Camera, May 27, 1930.
- Staff. "A Pretty Entertainment." *Boulder News,* January 13, 1897.
- Staff. "Boulder Women and Their Club." *Denver Sunday Times*, December 17, 1899.
- Staff. *Boulder* County Herald Weekly, December 30, 1896 and September 20, 1899.
- Staff. Boulder Daily Camera, May 11, 1894, February 20, 1895, August 20, 1895, February 15, 1896, June 27, 1896, and October 7 and 8, 1898.

- Staff. *Boulder* News, April 6, 1899.
- Staff. "University's Pay Roll." *Boulder Daily Camera*, November 23, 1896.
- Staff. *Boulder* County Herald Weekly, June 12, 1895.

Unpublished material and manuscripts include:

- Housel, Will, United States Civil Service Commission. Notice of Eligibility, July 5, 1899.
- Housel family records, in possession of Edgar Searles Housel.
- Rippon, Mary, diary, 1894 (January 17, December 29). Archives, University of Colorado at Boulder Libraries, Mary Rippon collection.
- Rippon, Mary, diary, 1895 (January 17, July 25–26). Archives, University of Colorado at Boulder Libraries, Mary Rippon collection.
- Rippon, Mary, diary, 1896 (February 1–4, February 25, March 24–May 15, June 25, July 17, December 5). Archives, University of Colorado at Boulder Libraries, Mary Rippon collection.
- Rippon, Mary, diary, accounting sections, 1892–1906. Archives, University of Colorado at Boulder Libraries, Mary Rippon collection.
- Rippon, Mary, land records, 1896, Book 176. Boulder County Clerk and Recorder, Boulder, Colorado.

Chapter 22

Book and magazine references include:

- Staff. *University* of Colorado Directory of Officers and Graduates, 1877–1921.
- Staff. *University of Colorado Bulletin*, Volume XXI #10, General Series #175, 1921.
- Woody, Thomas. *A History of Women's Education in the United States, Volume I.* Science Press, 1929, page 496.

Census references include:

- U.S. Census, Buffalo, Erie County, New York, 1900. (Will was a "tourist agent.")
- U.S. Census, Ann Arbor, Washtenaw County, Michigan, 1910.

Newspaper references include:

- Staff. *Boulder* News, March 29, 1900, and November 29, 1900.
- Staff. Boulder Daily Camera, March 19, 1900, and April 5, 1901.
- Staff. *Boulder* County Herald, December 12, 1900.

Unpublished material and manuscripts include:

- Baker, James H., to Rosetta Bell, May 21, 1902, in possession of Roland Wolcott. James H. Baker to Rosetta Bell, May 13, 1903.
- Housel, Will, diary, 1900, in possession of Robert P. Housel.
- Housel, Will, diary, August 25, 1900. (Will called his wife "Dorothy," not "Dora Mae.")
- Rippon, Mary, diary, 1900–1906, Archives, University of Colorado at Boulder Libraries, Mary Rippon collection.
- Rippon, Mary, diary, accounting section, 1900–1906.
- Rippon, Mary, to William C. Housel, land records, Liber 174, page 456, August 27, 1908. Washtenaw County Clerk, Ann Arbor, Michigan. (The warranty deed was for the east half of the northeast quarter of Section 8 in Pittsfield Township.)
- University of Colorado Regents' Minutes, April 21, 1900.
- University of Colorado Regents' Minutes, April 16, 1903.

Chapter 23

Book and magazine references include:

- Staff. *Coloradoan,* Volume IV, University of Colorado, 1903, pages 8–9.
- Staff. *Coloradoan,* Volume VII. University of Colorado, 1906, page 5.
- U.S. Bureau of the Census, "Historical Statistics of the U.S.," Government Printing Office, 1975.
- U.S. Bureau of the Census, "Statistical Abstracts of the U.S.," Government Printing Office, 1997.

Census references include:

- U.S. Census, Ann Arbor, Washtenaw County, Michigan, 1910.

Courthouse records include:

- Peter M. Housel, probate records, Case #1140, September 23, 1907, Colorado State Archives. (Sworn statement by Louisa Housel, "Peter M. Housel departed this life on or about April 17, 1905, leaving no last will and testament.")
- Mary Rippon to William C. Housel, land records, Liber 174, page 456, August 27, 1908. Washtenaw County Clerk, Ann Arbor, Michigan.

Newspaper references include:

- Staff. "She Mustn't Love," Boulder Daily Camera, September 9, 1904.
- Staff. Boulder Daily Camera, April 17, 1905 and March 23, 1906.

Unpublished material and manuscripts include:

- Green Mountain Cemetery records. Green Mountain Cemetery, Boulder, Colorado, 1905.
- Housel family records, in possession of Edgar Searles Housel.
- Rieder, Miriam Housel, student records. Office of the Registrar, University of Washington.
- Rippon, Mary, diary, accounting section, 1900–1906. Archives, University of Colorado at Boulder Libraries, Mary Rippon collection.

Chapter 24

Book and magazine references include:

- Davis, William E. *Glory* Colorado. Pruett Press, 1965, page 220.
- Staff. *Coloradoan.* Volume X. University of Colorado, 1909, page 15.

Newspaper references include:

- Staff. "Miss Rippon Resigns After Long Service." Boulder *Daily* Camera, July 14, 1909.

Unpublished material and manuscripts include:

- Rippon, Mary, to Rosetta Bell Wolcott, March 14, 1910, in possession of Roland Wolcott.
- Rippon, Mary, notations for the Carnegie Foundation. Archives, University of Colorado at Boulder Libraries, Mary Rippon collection.
- Thomas, Calvin, to Mary Rippon, June 1909. Archives, University of Colorado at Boulder Libraries, Mary Rippon collection.
- University of Colorado, Regents' Minutes, June 11, 1909.
- Wolcott, Rosetta Bell, diary, May 22, 1909. Archives, University of Colorado at Boulder Libraries, Rosetta Bell Wolcott collection.

Part 5: Retirement Years, 1909–1935
Chapter 25
Author's correspondence includes:

- re: Miriam Housel Rieder, student records, with Virjean Edwards (Office of the Registrar, University of Washington), September 11, 1998.
- re: Rudolf Rieder, employee records, with J. Frank Cook (University of Wisconsin, Madison, archives), September 9, 1997.
- re: Forest Hill Cemetery records, with David J. Brough, August 29, 1995.

Book and magazine references include:

- Anuta, Michael J. *Ships of Our Ancestors*. Genealogical Publishing Company, 1983, page 364.
- Davis, William E. *Glory* Colorado. Pruett Press, 1965, page 220.
- Felleman, Hazel, editor. *Best Loved Poems of the American People*. Garden City Books, 1936.
- Staff. *Silver* and Gold, Volume XVIII, September 16, 1909.

Census references include:

- U.S. Census, Hugo, Lincoln County, Colorado, 1920. ("Walfried W. Rieder, b. [born] Wisconsin.")
- U.S. Bureau of the Census, "Historical Statistics of the U.S.," Government Printing Office, 1975.
- U.S. Bureau of the Census, "Statistical Abstracts of the U.S.," Government Printing Office, 1997.

Newspaper references include:

- Staff. "Miss Rippon Resigns After Long Service." Boulder Daily Camera, July 14, 1909.
- Staff. "Hit By Auto and Died in Short Time." *The* Daily Times News, October 4, 1912.
- Staff. "Mrs. William Housel Died Sunday Night After Long Illness." *The* Daily Times News, May 20, 1912.
- Staff. "Says Housel Was to Blame for Killing." *Daily* Times News, October 6, 1912.
- Staff. "Wardwell Not to Blame Says Coroner Jury." *Daily* Times News, October 9, 1912.
- Staff. "Prof. Grace Baur of University of Colorado, Died Suddenly." Boulder Daily Camera, March 20, 1930.

Unpublished material and manuscripts include:

- Housel, Dorothy, obituary, uncited and undated (circa 1913) clipping, in possession of Edgar Searles Housel.
- Housel, Dorothy, Forest Hill Cemetery records. Deed 613-D, lot 26, block M, Ann Arbor, Michigan.
- Housel, Miriam, student records. University of Wisconsin archives, Madison, Wisconsin.
- Housel, Roy, diary, in possession of Robert P. Housel.
- Housel, William C., Forest Hill Cemetery records, Ann Arbor Michigan.

- Rieder, Miriam, list of degrees conferred. University of Washington Catalog, 1916.

- Rieder, Miriam, Passport application, August 23, 1916. National Archives.

- Rieder, Wilfred. "Introduction to Collection of Unpublished and Undated Manuscripts by Miriam Rieder." Archives, University of Colorado at Boulder Libraries, Miriam Rieder collection.

- Rippon, Mary, to Rosetta Wolcott, March 14, 1910, in possession of Roland Wolcott.

- Rippon, Mary, account books, 1909–1915 and 1916–1926. Archives, University of Colorado at Boulder Libraries, Mary Rippon collection.

Chapter 26

Author's correspondence and interviews include:

- Interview with Hortense Brant, October 21, 1996.

- Correspondence re: Rudolf Rieder, employee records, with J. Frank Cook (University of Wisconsin, Madison, archives), September 9, 1997.

Courthouse records include:

- William C. Housel, probate records. Liber 173, page 347. February 21, 1914, Washtenaw County Clerk, Ann Arbor, Washtenaw County, Michigan.

Newspaper references include:

- Staff. "Mrs. Miriam Rieder Dies After Long Illness." Boulder Daily Camera, September 27, 1957.

Unpublished material and manuscripts include:

- News Bureau form, Public Relations Department, University of Colorado, 1953, Miriam Rieder file.

- Rieder, Miriam to Roy, James, and Edgar Housel. December 2, 1913, in possession of Edgar Searles Housel.

- Rieder, Miriam. "Grasp That Torch," undated and unpublished manuscript. Archives, University of Colorado at Boulder Libraries, Miriam Rieder collection.

- Rieder, Miriam. "Journey Into Jeopardy," unpublished and undated manuscript. Archives, University of Colorado at Boulder libraries, Miriam Rieder collection.

- Rieder, Miriam, Passport application, August 23, 1916, with accompanying letter of August 22, 1916, National Archives.

- Rieder, Wilfred. "Introduction to unpublished manuscripts by Miriam Rieder." Archives, University of Colorado at Boulder libraries, Miriam Rieder collection.

- Rippon, Mary, diary, 1884 (October 12–21), Archives, University of Colorado at Boulder libraries, Mary Rippon collection.

- Rippon, Mary, account book, 1909–1915. Archives, University of Colorado at Boulder libraries, Mary Rippon collection.

- Rippon, Mary, to Ada Morris, February 10, 1919. Archives, University of Colorado at Boulder libraries, Ada Morris collection.

- Rippon, Mary, diary, December 25, 1917–January 8, 1918. Archives, University of Colorado at Boulder libraries, Mary Rippon collection.

Chapter 27

Author's correspondence and interviews include:

- Correspondence with E. Thomas Punshon, August 27, 1997.
- Interview with Nancy Atkins Ferriss, August 31, 1997.
- Correspondence with Dr. Ross Ingersoll, September 10, 1997.
- Telephone conversation with Alberta Nicholson, August 16, 1997.
- Interview with Joy Whitney Ahlborn, July 7, 1995.

Census references include:

- U.S. Census, Hugo, Lincoln County, Colorado, 1920.

Newspaper references include:

- Staff. *Denver* Times. January 18, 1917.
- Staff. Boulder *Daily* Camera, undated clipping, 1925.

Unpublished material and manuscripts include:

- News Bureau form, Public Relations Department, University of Colorado, 1953, Miriam Rieder file.
- Rieder, Miriam. "Grasp That Torch," undated and unpublished manuscript. Archives, University of Colorado at Boulder Libraries, Miriam Rieder collection.
- Rippon, Mary, account book, 1916–1926. Archives, University of Colorado at Boulder libraries, Mary Rippon collection.
- University of Colorado. "Directory of Officers and Graduates, 1877–1921."
- University of Colorado Bulletin, Volume XXI #10, General Series #175, 1921.
- University of Colorado, "Schedule of Courses, CU-College of Liberal Arts, 1920–1921." University of Colorado, 1921.

Chapter 28
Author's interviews include:

- Joy Whitney Ahlborn, July 7, 1995.
- Ardella Orton, June 26, 1998.

Book and magazine references include:

- Staff. "Miss Mary Rippon, Former Instructor in Colorado." *Colorado Alumnus,* Volume XVIII, February 1928, page 4.

Newspaper references include:

- Staff. "Some Sidelights on Fortnightly Club Celebrating Anniversary." Boulder *Daily* Camera, November 6, 1934.

- Staff. Boulder *Daily* Camera, November 22, 1926.
- Staff. "Dr. Norlin Repudiates a Scandal Story Published by Denver Post." Boulder *Daily* Camera, January 27, 1927.
- Staff. "Norlin Brands Love Scandal at Colorado U. as 'Idle Gossip.'" *Denver* Post, January 27, 1927.
- Staff. "Miss Mary Rippon Was Large Part of the U. of C." Boulder *Daily* Camera, November 4, 1927.
- Staff. "More Than 2,000 Present as University of Colorado Celebrates Half-Century of Progress in Education." *Rocky* Mountain News, November 4, 1927.
- Staff. "Whitney Is Dead." *Topeka Capital Journal*, August 31, 1925.

Unpublished material and manuscripts include:

- Envelope from Recorder of Deeds, St. Louis, Missouri, to Mrs. Miriam Rieder, March 14, 1927, in possession of Edgar Searles Housel.
- Graceland Cemetery records, Dominy Memorial Library, Fairbury, Illinois.
- Letterhead, Blue Front Cigar Store, Ann Arbor, Michigan, in possession of Edgar Searles Housel.
- Receipt from Miriam Rieder to V. E. Van Ameringen, March 25, 1927, in possession of Edgar Searles Housel.
- Rieder, Miriam, to Recorder of Deeds, St. Louis, Missouri, March 7, 1927, in possession of Edgar Searles Housel.
- Rippon, Mary, account books, 1916–1926 and 1927–1935. Archives, University of Colorado libraries, Mary Rippon collection.
- Rippon, Mary, Last Will and Testament, April 5, 1930, Colorado State Archives, Denver, Colorado.
- Title Insurance policy, Washtenaw Abstract Company, September 17, 1926, in possession of Edgar Searles Housel.

Chapter 29

Author's interviews include:

- Joy Whitney Ahlborn, July 7, 1995.

Newspaper references include:

- Staff. Boulder *Daily* Camera. October 3, 1934, and September 10, 1935.
- Staff. "Mary Rippon, Pioneer U. C. Teacher Dies." Boulder Daily Camera, September 9, 1935.
- Staff. "Whitney Is Dead," *Topeka Capital Journal*, August 31, 1925.

Unpublished material and manuscripts include:

- Final Report of the Administrator of the Account of Mary Rippon, Deceased. April 12, 1937, Colorado State Archives, Denver, Colorado.
- Rippon, Mary, Last Will and Testament, April 5, 1930. Colorado State Archives, Denver, Colorado.
- Waiver of Notice and Consent to Hearing and Admission of Will to Probate. October 1, 1935, Colorado State Archives.

Part 6: Mary Rippon Remembered, 1935–Present
Chapter 30
Book and magazine references include:

- Staff. "Dedication of the Theater." *Colorado Alumnus*, Volume XXVII, December 1936, pages 3–7.

Newspaper references include:

- Staff. "C. U. Plans Big Outdoor Theater as Memorial to Mary Rippon." Denver Post, February 29, 1936.

Unpublished material and manuscripts include:

- Berg, Louise, to the Mary Rippon Memorial Fund, September 12, 1935, and March 25, 1936. Archives, University of Colorado at Boulder libraries, Mary Rippon collection.
- Dakan, Jessie Stanton to Mary Rippon Memorial Fund, April 7, 1936. Archives, University of Colorado at Boulder libraries, Mary Rippon collection.

- Mary Rippon Memorial Fund receipt book. Archives, University of Colorado at Boulder libraries, Mary Rippon collection.
- University of Colorado Regents Minutes, February 28, 1936.
- Works Progress Administration Project Proposal, Project #1542 (65-84-2067) 10 March 1936. National Archives.

Chapter 31
Author's correspondence and interviews include:

- Correspondence with Dr. Ross Ingersoll, 1997 (August 31, September 5, September 10, and November 21, 1997).
- Correspondence with John Munro, November 11, 1997.
- Correspondence with Marilyn Reed, September 8, 1997.
- Interview with Nancy Atkins Ferris, August 31, 1997.
- Correspondence with Rosalie DeBacker Alldredge, September 1, 1997.
- Correspondence with Susan Huck Carpenter, November 19, 1997.
- Interview with Hortense Brant, November 10, 1997.
- Telephone interview with Louise Wicks, September 3, 1997.

Newspaper references include:

- Rieder, Miriam. "Open Forum," Boulder *Daily* Camera, February 27, 1947.
- Staff. Boulder *Daily* Camera, April 28, 1950 and May 5, 1950.
- Staff. Miriam Rieder, obituary. Boulder *Daily Camera*, September 27, 1957.

Unpublished material and manuscripts include:

- News Bureau form, Public Relations Department, University of Colorado, 1953. Miriam Rieder file.
- Rieder, Miriam to the editor of Boulder *Daily* Camera, undated. Boulder *Daily* Camera files.
- Rieder, Miriam Edna Housel, Social Security account application, October 25, 1955. Social Security Administration.

- Rieder, Miriam, Probate records #9122, filed March 29, 1958. Colorado State Archives.
- Rieder, Miriam, Death Certificate, September 27, 1957. Colorado Department of Health, Vital Records.

Chapter 32
Author's correspondence and interviews include:

- Interview with Cindy Carlisle, July 7, 2005, and correspondence March 27, 2023, and April 4, 2023.
- Interview with Michael L. Radelet, July 7, 2005, plus additional 2005–2006 correspondence.
- Correspondence with Dr. Adrian Del Caro, March 27, 2023.

Newspaper and magazine references include:

- Evans, Marty Coffin. "Fortnightly Continues a Rippon Tradition." *Coloradan:* The University of Colorado Alumni Magazine, June 2005.
- Pettem, Silvia. "The Secret Life of Mary Rippon." *Views* from CU-Boulder Colorado, August 1997.
- Pettem, Silvia. "Mary Rippon to Receive Posthumous Honorary Degree." Boulder *Daily* Camera, March 26, 2006.
- Resto-Montero, Gabriela. "Profs Honor Historic Female Instructor." *The* Campus Press, November 1–7, 2005.
- Talbott, Clint. "No Sheepskin for CU Trailblazer." Boulder *Daily* Camera, October 12, 2000.

Unpublished material and manuscripts include:

- Bartlett, Dr. Albert Allen. Support letter for Rippon's 1998 nomination, October 8, 1998.
- Bartlett, Dr. Albert Allen. Support letter for Rippon's 2005 nomination, October 29, 2005.
- Briggs, W. E. Support letter for Rippon's 1998 nomination, October 29, 1998.

- Chambers, Lee. Support comments via email to Michael L. Radelet, October 24, 2005.
- Del Caro, Dr. Adrian. Support letter for Rippon's 1998 nomination, October 9, 1998.
- Del Caro, Dr. Adrian. Support letter for Rippon's 2005 nomination, November 2, 2005.
- Hall, Wendy. Support letter for Rippon's 2005 nomination, September 9, 2005.
- Oltmans, Kay. Support letter for Rippon's 1998 nomination, October 30, 1998.
- Pettem, Silvia. Award Nomination Form, University of Colorado Honorary Degree, for Mary Rippon (deceased), November 4, 1998.
- Radelet, Michael L. Award Nomination Form, University of Colorado Honorary Degree, for Mary Rippon (deceased), November 15, 2005.
- Radelet, Michael L. Cover letter to the Board of Regents with 2005 Award Application, November 15, 2005.

Chapter 33
Author's correspondence and interviews include:

- Correspondence with Todd Gleeson, April 6, 2023.
- Correspondence with Julia Frey Nolet, July 20, 2022, February 20, 2023, and March 15, 2023.
- Correspondence with Michael L. Radelet, December 14, 2022.
- Interview with Michael L. Radelet, February 27, 2023.
- Correspondence with Eric Rieder, February 18, 2023, March 22, 2023, and April 7, 2023.

Unpublished material and manuscripts include:

- Nolet, Julia Frey. "Mary Rippon Endowed Scholarship Fund for Single Parents," August 31, 2020.

INDEX